DreamToys

Claire Garland

St. Martin's Griffin
New York

Contents

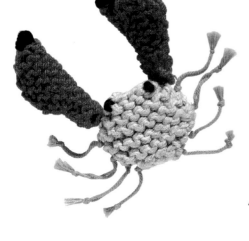

Dream maker

All young children have timeless spirit and the ability to be totally absorbed in an imaginary adventure. However, they do need a comforting playmate toy with which to share their triumphant 'today I sailed to sea and found the buried treasure' or 'tomorrow I'll be a beautiful princess and, and, and ...' fantasy. Because I look back affectionately to my primary-school years – romps through fields and forests, holidays by the seaside – I made this book an homage to all childhood wishes and dreams. It is an evocative makers' book that gives you the chance to create a special imagination tool for your young dreamer, and is a great way of using up leftover yarns. Knit a dream!

Knitting basics

Holding the needles and yarn

Knitters hold the needles and yarn in various ways. Try one of these three techniques to see which suits you best. Reverse the instructions if you are left-handed.

English method

While knitting, hold both needles from above between your left thumb, forefinger, and second finger, leaving the right hand to make the stitches. Hold the yarn on your right hand by passing it under and around the little finger, over the ring finger, under the second finger, and over the forefinger. Use your index finger to wind the working yarn over the tip of the needle to make the stitches, while your little finger controls the tension (the tightness/looseness) of the yarn and therefore the neatness of the knitting.

Continental method

Hold the needles as you would with the English method only this time wrap the yarn around your left little finger and over the top of the left forefinger. Use the right-hand needle to make the stitches, while controlling the tension with your left hand.

French method

Wrap the yarn around your fingers as for the English method but hold the right-hand needle from below as you would a pencil. Use your right forefinger to guide the working yarn.

Slip knot

Most knitting starts with a slip knot, which becomes the very first stitch on the needle.

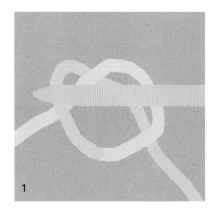

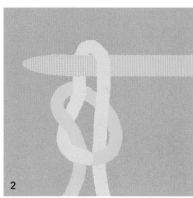

1 Leave a long tail of yarn. Wind the working yarn around your left index finger from front to back and around to the back again. Slide the circle of yarn off the finger and push a loop of working yarn through the circle from back to front. Push the tip of one needle through the loop and pull the slip knot up.

2 Pull the loose tail of yarn down away from the needle to tighten the knot, although not too tightly. Pull the working yarn if you need to slacken the knot.

Casting on

Here are two methods of casting on –
have a go at both then see which one
you feel most comfortable with.

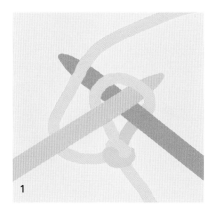

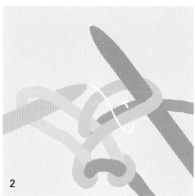

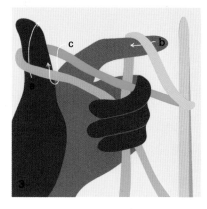

1st method

1 Holding the yarn at the back of the
   left-hand needle, insert the tip of the
   right-hand needle into the slip knot
   from the front to the back. With the
   working yarn in your right hand, pass
   it from the back of the work to the
   front around the tip of the right-hand
   needle as shown.

2 With the left-hand needle still in the
   slip knot, draw the right-hand needle
   and the working yarn forwards
   through the slip knot to make a loop
   on the right-hand needle. Slip the
   loop onto the left-hand needle as
   shown by the arrow.

3 Remove the right-hand needle. You
   have now cast on two stitches.

To cast on more stitches, insert the
right-hand needle into the front of the
second stitch and then repeat from step
1. Continue to make stitches in the
same way until you have the required
number on the needle.

   Now you can begin to knit or purl
rows to create the knitted textile.

2nd method

1 Put the yarn from the short end of
   the yarn around your thumb and the
   yarn from the ball of yarn around
   your forefinger as shown above.

2 Take two needles in your right hand,
   and insert the tip of the needles
   under the yarn, between the thumb
   and forefinger as shown.

3 Insert the needle up through the
   loop on your thumb (a), around the
   loop on your index finger (b), and
   through the center of the loop on
   your thumb (c) so that the yarn
   around the forefinger is drawn
   through the yarn on your thumb.
   Let the yarn slip off your thumb
   and again place the end of the
   yarn around your thumb.

Continue to make stitches in the same
way until you have the required number
on the needle.

   Now you can begin to knit or purl
rows to create the knitted textile.

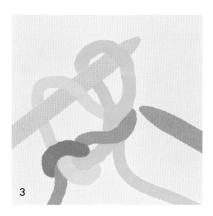

Knitting basics

Knit (K)

A knitted row is usually the right side of the textile. Knitting every row produces garter stitch.

Purl (P)

Alternating purled and knitted rows is called stocking/stockinette stitch. Here are two methods to choose from.

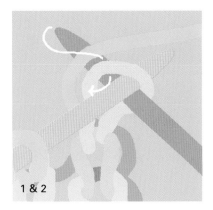

1 & 2

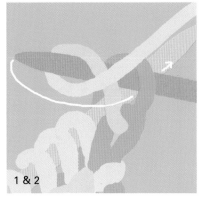

1 & 2

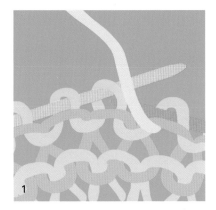

1

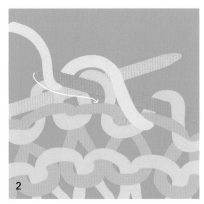

2

1 With the cast-on stitches on the left-hand needle, insert the tip of the right-hand needle into the first stitch from the front to the back. Holding the working yarn at the back of the needles, bring it around the tip of the right-hand needle, so it is in between the right- and left-hand needles.

2 Draw the yarn forwards through the stitch on the left-hand needle to make a new stitch on the right-hand needle. Slip the original stitch off the left-hand needle. Continue knitting in this way into each cast-on stitch, until they have all been knitted onto the right needle.

1st Method

1 Hold the needle with the stitches in your left hand and the yarn in the right hand. Holding the working yarn at the front of the work, insert the right-hand needle through the first stitch on the left-hand needle from the back to the front. Wind the working yarn over the top of the right-hand needle from the right to the left.

2 Draw the yarn through the stitch on the left-hand needle to make a new stitch on the right-hand needle. Slip the original stitch off the left-hand needle. Continue purling in the same way to the end of the row.

2nd Method

1 Place the yarn on the left hand and left forefinger. Holding the working yarn at the front of the work, insert the tip of the right-hand needle into the stitch from right to left.

2 Twist the left-hand needle up and around the yarn, then pull the yarn through the stitch. Let the original stitch slip of the left needle.

Increase (inc)

To add a stitch to the row, knit (purl) into the front and then the back of a stitch to increase one stitch. This is abbreviated as Kfb (Pfb).

Decrease (dec)

This technique makes the width of the textile narrower and is used for shaping.

Casting off

This is the way to finish your piece of knitting so that it does not unravel.

1 & 2

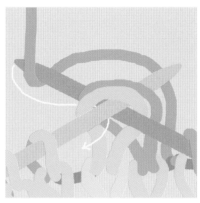

1, 2, & 3

1 Work to where the extra stitch is needed. Knit or purl through the front of the stitch but do not drop it off the left-hand needle.

2 With the yarn at the back of the work, and slip the tip of the right-hand needle through the back of the stitch still on the left-hand needle, and knit or purl another stitch. Slip the original stitch off the left-hand needle.

On a knit row
Insert the tip of the right-hand needle from left to right into the second stitch (see above) and then the first stitch on the left-hand needle, then knit the two stitches together to make one stitch

On a purl row (not illustrated)
Insert the right-hand needle from right to left through the first two stitches on the left-hand needle, then purl them together to make one stitch.

1 Knit or purl the first two stitches according to the pattern, so that two stitches are on the right-hand needle.

2 Use the tip of the left-hand needle to lift the first stitch (illustrated as a white outline), then pass it over the second stitch and off the needle. Knit or purl the next stitch on the left-hand needle. Repeat from the beginning of this step until one stitch remains.

3 Pull the last stitch to tighten it. Break off or cut the working yarn, leaving a long end for sewing the seams later. Thread the end through the last stitch and pull it to tighten it.

Crochet basics

Slip knot

Almost all crochet starts with a slip knot – the very first stitch on the hook.

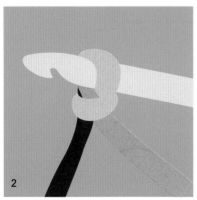

1 Leaving a long tail of yarn, loop the yarn as shown above, crossing the ball end over the tail end. Insert the hook through the loop catching the yarn attached to the ball.

2 Pull the yarn through to make a loop. Gently tighten the loop knot and slide it up the hook.

Make chain (ch)

These next steps direct you how make the first group of chains upon which the crochet will be worked. Each crochet pattern will instruct you how many chain to make to begin.

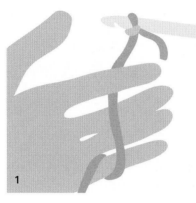

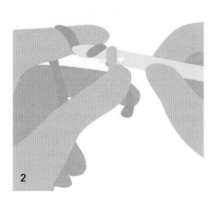

1 Wrap the yarn from the ball around the little finger of your left hand, then allow it lie under the forefinger. This will help you maintain an even tension as you crochet. Hold the hook in your right hand as you would a pencil or as you would a knife – however you feel comfortable. The hook should be facing downwards.

2 Keep the yarn taut and use the forefinger of the left hand to place the yarn around the lip of the hook.

Then pull the yarn around the hook through the loop on the hook.

To make the number of chains required in the pattern, repeat step 2. You can count them easily as each one forms a neat chain loop.

Slip Stitch (ss)

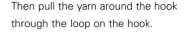

Slip stitch or single crochet is used in the projects to join the end and the beginning of a round.

1 With the crocheted chain held taut between your thumb and middle finger of your left hand, and the working yarn over your forefinger, insert the hook into the second chain from the hook. Wrap the yarn around the hook and draw a new loop through both loops on the hook (as shown by the arrow). This leaves one loop remaining on the hook. One slip stitch has been made.

Double crochet (dc)/US single crochet (sc)

This is the easiest of all the crochet stitches, and the one that is used for the majority of the projects in this book.

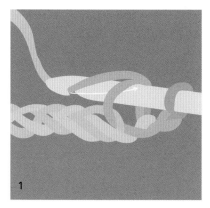

1

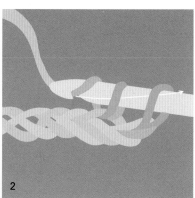

2

1   With the crocheted chain held taut between your thumb and middle finger of your left hand, and the yarn over your forefinger, insert the hook into the second chain from the hook as you began with the slip stitch. Wrap the yarn around the hook and draw a new loop through the chain. This leaves two loops remaining on the hook.

2   Wrap the yarn around the hook and pull a loop through both loops on the hook. One loop remains on the hook. One double crochet has been made.

Repeat steps 1 and 2 in each chain to the last chain to complete one row of double crochet (1 row dc).
To make more rows of double crochet, turn the work so that the hook is at the opposite edge of the last row. Make one chain stitch then insert the hook into both loops of the first double crochet of the last row, to make the first double crochet. Work a double crochet into each double crochet in this way.

Treble crochet (tr)/US double crochet (dc)

Working treble crochet results in a more open texture than double crochet. It was used in the Mustang Blanket project to create an open design.

1   With the crocheted chain held taut between your thumb and middle finger of your left hand, and the working yarn over your forefinger, wrap the yarn around the hook and insert the hook into the fourth chain from the hook.

2   Pull a loop through this chain only so there are three loops on the hook. Wrap the yarn around the hook again and pull a new loop through the first two loops on the hook. Two loops are now on the hook.

3   Wrap the yarn around the hook again (a third time), then pull a new loop through both loops on the hook. One treble has been made. Make more in the same way.

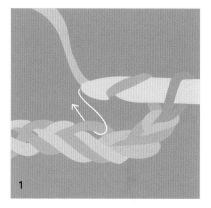

1

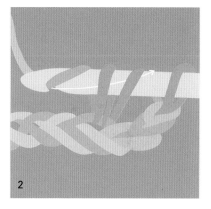

2

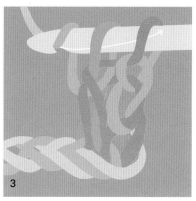

3

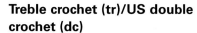

Crochet basics

Working in rounds

To create a circular piece, you can work crochet in rounds rather than rows. The initial chain row is made into a ring and this becomes the foundation on which the circular piece is worked.

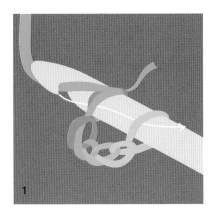

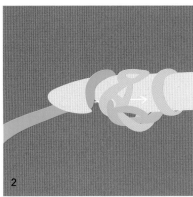

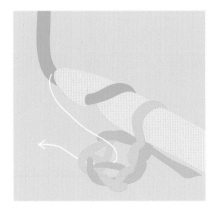

1 Make a length of chain as directed in the pattern. Then join this into a ring with a slip stitch. Insert the hook into the first chain made, wrap the yarn around the hook and draw a new loop through both loops on the hook. This forms a ring of chain stitches.

To work double crochet (dc)/US single crochet (sc) into the ring *(see below)*

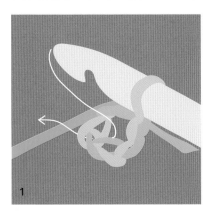

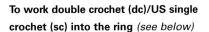

1 Insert the hook, front to back, through the center of the ring. Wrap the yarn around the hook (at the back of the ring) in the direction shown.

2 Draw a new loop back through the ring. This leaves two loops remaining on the hook.

3 Wrap the yarn around the hook and pull a loop through both loops on the hook. One loop remains on the hook. One double crochet has been made into the ring. Continue making as many double crochet into the ring as the pattern directs. From here on the crochet is worked in rounds around the edge of the ring into each stitch. It is always a good tip to lay a strand of yarn over the last/first stitch as a marker at the beginning of each round to determine where you started.

To work treble crochet (tr)/US double crochet (dc) into the ring *(see above)*
Wrap the yarn around the hook first, insert the wrapped hook into the ring and then draw a new loop back through the ring. Complete the treble in the usual way. Make as many treble into the ring as instructed.

 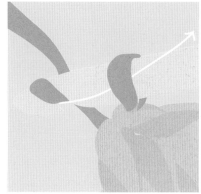

Adding on new yarn

You will need to join in new yarn if
your first ball of yarn runs out or if
you wish to add a new color.

Insert the hook into the crochet at
the point desired, wrap the new yarn
over it, and simply pull a loop through,
leaving a tail of about 10cm/4in.
Continue with the crochet as required.
Weave in any loose ends when the
crochet has been completed.

To fasten off

This is the way to finish your
crochet at the end of a piece
to stop it unravelling.

When you have reached the end of
the pattern, cut the yarn about 10cm/4in
from the work, pull the tail end through
the loop on the hook, and pull tight.
Weave in any loose ends on the wrong
side of the piece.

Stitching basics

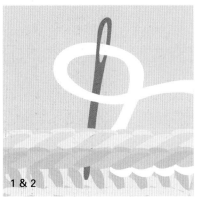

1 & 2

Mattress stitch

Also known as invisible seaming, this is widely used for joining side and sleeve seams on knitting, or where a flat seam is required.

1 Place the two pieces to be joined side by side, right sides up, matching stitch for stitch. Thread a blunt-ended yarn needle with a length of matching yarn. Bring the needle out through the center of the first stitch, just above the cast-off edge on one piece. Slip the needle through the center of the corresponding stitch on the other piece and out through the center of the stitch above. Then insert the needle through the center of the first stitch on the first piece again and out through the center of the stitch above it. Continue in this way along the whole seam.

Backstitch

This method is good for firm seams on both knitting and crochet.

1 Place the two pieces to be joined right sides together and pin the edges together, matching stitch for stitch. Thread a blunt-ended yarn needle with a length of matching yarn. Work from right to left. Bring the yarn to the front of the work, one stitch in from both adjacent edges. Insert the needle from the front to the back through the layers and back through to the front, one stitch to the left of the original stitch.

2 Insert the needle through the layers two stitches to the right, at the end of the previous stitch and back through to the front again four stitches to the left. Repeat from the beginning of this step until the seam has been completed along the edge.

Sew in each loose end by threading it onto a needle and working running stitch along the edge of the item. Oversew to secure the thread.

Swiss darning/duplicate stitch

This is a simple way to add a pattern over the top of finished stocking/stockinette stitch. Work from the chart, reading each square as one Swiss-darned/duplicate stitch.

Thread a blunt-ended yarn sewing needle with the appropriate colored yarn and bring it up through the middle of a knitted stitch, leaving a long end at the back. Darn an embroidered stitch over the top of each stocking stitch. Weave in all the loose ends at the back of the knitting when the embroidery is complete.

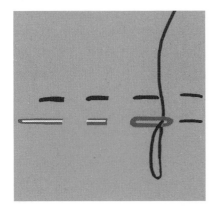

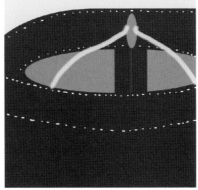

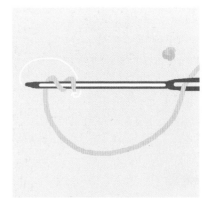

Running stitch

These neat stitches can be used for sewing seams or as a decorative top stitch.

Secure the thread and sew small even stitches along the line.

Making a casing

Use this method for creating a casing for elastic or a drawstring, for example around a waist.

Fold the casing allowance to the wrong side and then fold under the raw edge. Sew the casing in place along both folded edges with running stitch. Leave an opening in the bottom line of stitching or, if the casing runs across a seam, carefully unpick the wrong side of the seam between the two rows of stitches. Thread the elastic or drawstring through the casing, using a safety pin. Join the ends securely and let them slide inside the casing. Slip stitch the casing closed.

French knot

Lying like a bead on the fabric, a French knot is decorative and textural.

Bring the needle and thread through to the front. Wind the thread two or three times around the tip of the needle. Keeping the coils taut, re-insert the needle close to where the thread first emerged. Pull the thread through, making sure the knot holds its shape. Secure the thread at the back.

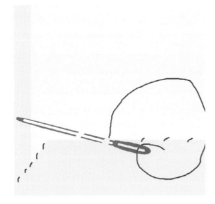

Slip stitch

Use this stitch to secure a folded edge in place on your fabric, as on a hem.

Secure the thread in the fold and work from right to left. Slide the needle through the folded edge, then make an almost invisible stitch by picking up a few threads in the fabric you are stitching it to. Continue in this way.

Abbreviations and needle sizes

BELOW ARE EXPLAINED THE ABBREVIATIONS USED IN THE BOOK, NEEDLE AND HOOK SIZES, AND UK AND US TERMINOLOGY.

Knitting abbreviations

The abbreviations below are the general ones used in the knitting patterns in this book. Any special abbreviations are given within the individual patterns.

alt	alternate
beg	begin(ning)
cm	centimetre(s)
cont	continu(e)(ing)
dec	decreas(e)(ing)
DK	double knitting (a medium-weight yarn)
foll	follow(s)(ing)
g	gram(s)
in	inch(es)
inc	increas(e)(ing); increase one st by working into front and back of st
K	knit
K2tog	knit next 2 sts together
Kfb	knit into front and back of next st
k-wise	knitwise
mm	millimetre(s)
oz	ounce(s)
P	purl
P2tog	purl next 2 sts together
patt	pattern; or work in pattern
Pfb	purl into front and back of next st
p-wise	purlwise
rem	remain(s)(ing)
rev st st	reverse stocking/stockinette st; purl RS rows and knit WS rows
rep	repeat(s)(ing)
RS	right side
st(s)	stitch(es)
st st	stocking/stockinette stitch; knit RS rows and purl WS rows
tog	together
WS	wrong side
yfwd	yarn forward (US yo)

* Repeat instructions after asterisk or between asterisks as many times as instructed.

[ ] Repeat instructions inside square brackets as many times as instructed.

Crochet abbreviations and terms

The crochet patterns in this book are written with UK crochet terminology. US terminology is given below for the UK techniques used in this book. Any abbreviations that are common to both knitting and crochet are listed in the knitting abbreviations.

UK	US
ch chain	**ch** chain
dc double crochet	**sc** single crochet
miss	**skip**
ss slip stitch	**slip st** slip stitch
tr treble	**dc** double crochet
yrh yarn around hook	**yo** yarn over (or around) hook

UK and US knitting terminology

The knitting patterns in this book are written with UK terminology. The differences in UK and US terminology are as follows:

UK	US
cast off	bind off
DK-weight yarn	light worsted-weight yarn
4-ply-weight yarn	fingering-weight yarn
moss stitch	seed stitch
stocking stitch	stockinette stitch
Swiss darning	duplicate stitch
tension	gauge
work straight	work even

Needle and hook conversion charts

This chart shows how different knitting-needle and crochet-hook systems compare. Where there is no exact match, the closest size is used as the equivalent. Always check your needle or hook size by knitting or crocheting a tension swatch before beginning a project. Only the range of sizes that might be of help with the toys are listed here.

Crochet hooks

METRIC	US	OLD UK
2.50mm	C/2	12
3.00mm	D/3	10
3.50mm	E/4	9
4.00mm	F/5	8
4.50mm	G/6	7
5.00mm	H/8	6
5.50mm	I/9	5

Knitting needles

METRIC	US	OLD UK
2¼mm	1	13
2¾mm	2	12
3mm		11
3¼mm	3	10
3½mm	4	
3¾mm	5	9
4mm		8
4½mm	7	7
5mm	8	6

Basic doll

This is the basic pattern for the dolls in the book. Refer back to this pattern when knitting them.

Finished size
For size of completed doll, see individual patterns.

Yarn
Doll: 4-ply-weight (US fingering-weight) wool, cotton, or mixed-fiber yarn in main color MC
Hair: A medium- or heavy-weight wool, cotton, or mixed-fiber yarn in A
For specific yarns and yarn amounts, see individual patterns.

Fabric and extras
Felt: Scraps of felt in 3 colors, for outer eyes, inner eyes, and mouth
Embroidery thread: Stranded cotton, for sewing on eyes and mouth, and embroidering nose
Filling: Polyester toy filling
For specific fabric and thread colors, see individual patterns.

Needles
Pair of 2¾mm (US 2) knitting needles
Blunt-ended yarn sewing needle
Embroidery sewing needle

Tension/gauge
30 sts and 38 rows to 10cm/4in measured over st st using 2¾mm (US size 2) needles and yarn MC. (Cowboy on pages 64–69 is worked in a thicker yarn, so it has a different tension/gauge).

Front
Front of doll body and head are worked in one piece, starting at beginning of body as foll:
Body
Using 2¾mm (US size 2) needles and yarn MC (skin color), cast on 18 sts.
Place *marker* on 3rd and 15th cast-on sts to mark outside thigh position for each leg.
Beg with a K row, work 36 rows in st st, so ending with a WS row.
Shape shoulders and neck
Next row (dec row) (RS) K2tog, K to last 2 sts, K2tog. (16 sts)
Next row (dec row) P2tog, P to last 2 sts, P2tog. (14 sts)
Place marker at each end of last row for underarm positions.
Rep last 2 rows once more. (10 sts)
Next row (dec row) K2tog, K to last 2 sts, K2tog. (8 sts)
Beg with a P row, work straight in st st for 3 rows, so ending with a WS row.
Shape head
Girl doll (Princess on pages 32–35 and Fairy on pages 44–51) and boy doll (Cowboy on pages 64–69 and Pirate on pages 76–85) have slightly different head shapes (see pages 21 and 22).

Girl doll only:
Next row (inc row) (RS) Cast on 1 st, K to last st, K into front and back of st to inc one st—called *Kfb*. (10 sts)
Next row (inc row) Cast on 1 st, P to last st, P into front and back of st to inc one st—called *Pfb*. (12 sts)
Rep last 2 rows 4 times more, so ending with a WS row. (28 sts)
Beg with a K row, work straight in st st for 15 rows, so ending with a RS row.
Next row (dec row) (WS) *P2tog, rep from * to end. (14 sts)
Knit 1 row.
Next row (dec row) *P2tog, rep from * to end. (7 sts)
Cast off.

Boy doll only:
Next row (inc row) (RS) Cast on 1 st, K to last st, K into front and back of st to inc one st—called *Kfb*. (10 sts)
Purl 1 row.
Next row (inc row) Cast on 1 st, K to last st, Kfb. (12 sts)
Next row (inc row) Cast on 1 st, P to last st, P into front and back of st to inc one st—called *Pfb*. (14 sts)
Rep last 2 rows 3 times more, so ending with a WS row. (26 sts)
Next row (inc row) (RS) Cast on 1 st, K to last st, Kfb. (28 sts)
Beg with a P row, work straight in st st

for 15 rows, so ending with a WS row.

Next row (dec row) (RS) *K2tog, rep from * to end. (14 sts)

Purl 1 row.

Next row (dec row) *K2tog, rep from * to end. (7 sts)

Cast off p-wise.

Back

Work exactly as for front.

Arms (make 2)

Using 2¾mm (US size 2) needles and yarn MC, cast on 4 sts.

Beg with a K row, work in st st until arm measures 20cm/8in from cast-on edge, ending with a WS row.

Cast off.

(Arms curl into tubes naturally and do not need seaming).

Legs (make 2)

Using 2¾mm (US size 2) needles and yarn MC, cast on 6 sts.

Beg with a K row, work in st st until leg measures 24cm/9½in from cast-on edge, ending with a WS row.

Cast off.

(Legs curl into tubes naturally and do not need seaming.)

To make up

Press front and back of doll lightly on wrong side, following instructions on yarn label. Do NOT press arms and legs. Sew on eyes, nose, and mouth before stitching knitted pieces together.

Eyes

Cut out felt pieces for outer and inner eyes, using templates (see page 110). Using two strands of stranded cotton and an embroidery sewing needle, sew each inner eye to center of an outer eye with a French knot. Using two strands of stranded cotton and working short straight stitches, sew inner eyes in place, then sew eyes to face on doll front.

Mouth and nose

Follow instructions for individual dolls for mouth and nose.

Body and head

With right sides together and using a blunt-ended yarn needle and matching yarn, sew back of doll to front with backstitches, leaving an opening at bottom edge for turning right side out. Turn right side out and lightly fill doll with toy filling.

Overcast stitch opening closed.

Arms

Weave in cast-on and cast-off yarn ends on each arm to neaten. Sew cast-on edge of each arm to body at an

underarm marker, with row ends curled in on underside of arm.

Legs

Weave in cast-on and cast-off yarn ends on each leg to neaten. Sew cast-off edge of each leg to body at a leg marker, with row ends curled in towards back.

Hair

For strands of hair, cut lengths of yarn A twice as long as desired finished length of hair, or as described in pattern. Work hair as a hairpiece *or* attach it in individual tufts or strands (see above). Tufted hair method works well with mohair and hairpiece method with thicker yarns. Work as follows:

Hairpiece: Thread a length of yarn A onto a blunt-ended yarn needle and use this to join strands of hair together. Insert needle through strand of hair (at center of strand for a center hair parting). Slide strand of hair along length of A on needle. To complete a hair piece, continue adding strands of hair in this way onto length of yarn on needle. Space the strands out along the foundation strand, don't bunch them together. Hair parting is formed along line where hair strands are threaded onto length of yarn on needle. When hairpiece is ready, sew it to top of doll's head with backstitch along center hair parting. Catch in a couple of strands at side of head to hold hair in place. Alternatively, sew on hairpiece with foundation strand running along head seam, from ear to ear, then cut hair at front to form a fringe.

Tufts of hair: Use six strands of yarn A (mohair) together for each tuft of hair. Align group of six strands, fold them in half, thread fold through a blunt-ended yarn needle and slide needle along to opposite end of yarn. Beginning at top of head next to head seam, insert needle in and out, and as needle emerges pass it through loop at folded end of strands. Pull loop down to top of head to secure, then slip off needle. Sew on tufts of hair like this all along what will be hairline – from ear to ear. Work two or more rows across back of head until the desired effect is achieved.

Basic horse

This is the basic pattern for the horses in the book. Refer to this pattern when knitting them.

Finished size
Completed toy measures approximately 40cm/15¾in long x 36cm/14¼in tall.

Yarn
Horse: A DK-weight (US light-worsted-weight) wool, cotton, or mixed-fiber yarn in main color MC

Muzzle and hooves: A DK-weight (US light-worsted-weight) yarn wool, cotton, or a mixed-fiber yarn in A

Mane and tail: A lightweight mohair in B
For specific yarns and yarn amounts, see individual patterns.

Fabric and extras
Felt: Scraps of felt in 3 colors, for outer and inner eyes and nostrils

Embroidery thread: Stranded cotton, for sewing on eyes and nostrils

Filling: Polyester toy filling
For specific fabric and thread colors, see individual patterns.

Needles
Pair of 3¾mm (US size 5) knitting needles
Blunt-ended yarn sewing needle
Embroidery sewing needle

Tension/gauge
22 sts and 30 rows to 10cm/4in measured over st st using 3¾mm (US size 5) needles and yarn MC.

Basic horse

Horse head and body

Horse head and body are worked in one piece, starting at muzzle-end as foll:
Using 3¾mm (US size 5) needles and yarn A (muzzle and hoof color), cast on 6 sts, leaving a long tail end.

Shape muzzle

Work muzzle in rev st st as foll:

Row 1 (RS) P to end.

Row 2 (inc row) (WS) *K into front and back of st to inc one st—called *Kfb*—, rep from * to end (to inc into every st). (12 sts)

Row 3 (inc row) *P into front and back of st to inc one st—called *Pfb*—, rep from * to end (to inc into every st). (24 sts)

Row 4 K to end.

Row 5 (inc row) *P1, Pfb, rep from * to end. (36 sts)

Beg with a K row, work straight in rev st st for 12 rows, so ending with a *RS* (P) row.

Row 18 (dec row) (WS) K2tog, K1, K2tog, K to last 5 sts, K2tog, K1, K2tog. (32 sts)

Break off yarn A.

Shape head

Now change to st st and yarn MC (horse color) and cont as foll:
Beg with a K row, work straight in st st for 2 rows, so ending with a WS row.

Row 21 (inc row) (RS) K10, Kfb, K to last 11 sts, Kfb, K10. (34 sts)

Beg with a P row, work straight in st st for 3 rows, so ending with a WS row.

Row 25 (inc row) (RS) K9, Kfb, K to last 10 sts, Kfb, K9. (36 sts)

Purl 1 row.

Row 27 (inc row) Kfb, K to last st, Kfb. (38 sts)

Purl 1 row.

Rep last 2 rows 4 times more, so ending with a WS row. (46 sts)

Shape neck

Row 37 (RS) Cast off 14 sts, K to last 14 sts, cast off last 14 sts and fasten off. (18 sts)

With WS facing, rejoin yarn MC to rem 18 sts and purl 1 row.

Row 39 (inc row) Kfb, K to last st, Kfb. (20 sts)

Place *marker* on 4th st from each end of last row for positions of ears.

Row 40 (inc row) Pfb, P to last st, Pfb. (22 sts)

Rep last 2 rows 4 times more, so ending with a WS row. (38 sts)

Row 49 (inc row) (RS) Kfb, K to last st, Kfb. (40 sts)

Beg with a P row, work straight in st st for 5 rows, so ending with a WS row.

Row 55 (shaping row) (RS) Kfb, K18, K2tog (2 center sts), K to last st, Kfb. (41 sts)

Row 56 (inc row) Pfb, P to last st, Pfb. (43 sts)

Place a *marker* at each end of last row for position of beg of underside of neck.

Row 57 (shaping row) Kfb, K20, cast off 1 st (center st), K to last st, Kfb. (44 sts)

Row 58 (inc row) Pfb, P to last st, Pfb. (46 sts)

Row 59 (shaping row) (RS) Kfb, K21, K2tog (2 center sts), K to last st, Kfb. (47 sts)

Row 60 (inc row) Pfb, P to last st, Pfb. (49 sts)

Row 61 (shaping row) Kfb, K23, cast off 1 st (center st), K to last st, Kfb. (50 sts)

Row 62 (inc row) Pfb, P to last st, Pfb. (52 sts)

Row 63 (shaping row) (RS) Kfb, K24, K2tog, K to last st, Kfb. (53 sts)

Row 64 (inc row) Pfb, P to last st, Pfb. (55 sts)

Row 65 (shaping row) Kfb, K26, cast off 1 st, K to last st, Kfb. (56 sts)

Row 66 (inc row) Pfb, P to last st, Pfb. (58 sts)

Row 67 (shaping row) (RS) Kfb, K27, K2tog, K to last st, Kfb. (59 sts)

Row 68 (inc row) Pfb, P to last st, Pfb. (61 sts)

Row 69 (shaping row) Kfb, K29, cast off 1 st, K to last st, Kfb. (62 sts)

Row 70 (inc row) Pfb, P to last st, Pfb. (64 sts)

Shape shoulders

Row 71 K3, Kfb, *K2, Kfb, rep from * to last 3 sts, K3. (84 sts)

Beg with a P row, work straight in st st for 7 rows, so ending with a WS row.

Row 79 (dec row) (RS) *K2, K2tog, rep from * to end of row. (63 sts)

Purl 1 row.

Shape back

Row 81 *K2, K2tog, rep from * to last 3 sts, K3. (48 sts)

Beg with a P row, work straight in st st for 11 rows, so ending with a WS row.

Shape haunches

Row 93 (inc row) (RS) K3, Kfb, *K5, Kfb, rep from * to last 2 sts, K2. (56 sts)

Purl 1 row.

Row 95 (inc row) K3, Kfb, *K6, Kfb, rep from * last 3 sts, K3. (64 sts)

Purl 1 row.

Row 97 (inc row) K4, Kfb, *K7, Kfb, rep from * to last 3 sts, K3. (72 sts)

Purl 1 row.

Row 99 (inc row) K4, Kfb, *K8, Kfb, rep from * to last 4 sts, K4. (80 sts)

Purl 1 row.

Row 101 (inc row) K5, Kfb, *K9, Kfb, rep from * to last 4 sts, K4. (88 sts)

Beg with a P row, work straight in st st for 13 rows, so ending with a WS row.

Shape end of body

Row 115 (dec row) (RS) K1, K2tog,

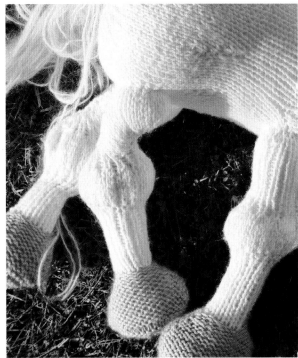

*K10, K2tog, rep from * to last st, K1. (80 sts)

Purl 1 row.

Row 117 (dec row) *K2tog, rep from * to end. (40 sts)

Beg with a P row, work straight in st st for 3 rows, so ending with a WS row. Rep last 4 rows once more. (20 sts)

Row 125 (dec row) (RS) *K2tog, rep from * to end. (10 sts)

Break off yarn leaving a long tail-end, then thread yarn end onto a blunt-ended yarn needle and pass yarn needle through sts as they are slipped off knitting needle. Pull tight to gather sts and secure with a few sts.

Ears (make 2)

Using 3¾mm (US size 5) needles and yarn MC (horse color), cast on 8 sts, leaving a long tail-end.

Work in st st as foll:
Purl 1 row.

Next row (RS) K2tog, K to last 2 sts, K2tog. (6 sts)

Rep last 2 rows once more, so ending with a *RS* row. (4 sts)

Beg with a P row, work straight in st st for 9 rows, so ending with a WS row.

Next row (RS) (K2tog) twice. (2 sts)

Cast off p-wise, leaving a long tail-end.

Forelegs (make 2)

Forelegs are started at hoof end as foll:
Using 3¾mm (US size 5) needles and yarn A (muzzle and hoof color), cast on 4 sts.

Shape base of hoof

Beg hoof in rev st st as foll:

Row 1 (WS) *Kfb, rep from * to end (to inc k-wise into every st). (8 sts)

Row 2 P to end.

Rep last 2 rows twice more. (32 sts)

Work 3 rows in garter st (knit every row). (Center row of garter st forms edge of base of hoof.)

Shape front of hoof

Purl 1 row.

Row 11 (inc row) (WS) K15, [Kfb] twice, K to end. (34 sts)

Purl 1 row.

Row 13 (dec row) K16, K2tog, K to end. (33 sts)

Row 14 (dec row) P16, cast off next st, P to end. (32 sts)

Row 15 (dec row) K15, K2tog, K to end. (31 sts)

Row 16 (dec row) P2tog, P to center st, cast off 1 st (center st), P to last 2 sts, P2tog. (28 sts)

Row 17 (dec row) K2tog, K to center 2 sts, K2tog, K to last 2 sts, K2tog. (25 sts)

Basic horse

Rep last 2 rows twice more, so ending with a WS row. (13 sts)
Break off yarn A.

Begin leg
Now change to st st and yarn MC (horse color) and cont as foll:
Beg with a K (RS) row, work straight in st st for 16 rows, so ending with a WS row.

Shape knee joint
Row 38 (inc row) (RS) K1, *Kfb, K1, rep from * to end. (19 sts)
Purl 1 row.
Row 40 (inc row) *Kfb, rep from * to end. (38 sts)
Beg with a P row, work straight in st st for 5 rows, so ending with a WS row.
Row 46 (dec row) (RS) *K1, K2tog, rep from * to last 2 sts, K2. (26 sts)
Row 47 (dec row) *P2tog, rep from * to end. (13 sts)**

Top of leg
Beg with a K row, work straight in st st for 14 rows, so ending with a WS row.
Row 62 (inc row) Kfb, K to last st, Kfb. (15 sts)
Purl 1 row.
Row 64 (inc row) K1, Kfb, *K2, Kfb, rep from * to last st, K1. (20 sts)
Purl 1 row.
Row 66 (inc row) K2, *Kfb, K2, rep from * to end. (26 sts)
Cast off p-wise, leaving a long tail-end.

Hind legs (make 2)
Work as for foreleg to **. (13 sts)
Knit 1 row.
Row 49 (inc row) P5, [Pfb] 3 times, P5. (16 sts)

Shape leg
Row 50 (shaping row) K2tog, K4, [Kfb] 4 times, K to last 2 sts, K2tog. (18 sts)
Row 51 (shaping row) P2tog, P5, [Pfb] 4 times, P to last 2 sts, P2tog. (20 sts)

Row 52 (shaping row) K2tog, K6, [Kfb] 4 times, K to last 2 sts, K2tog. (22 sts)
Row 53 (shaping row) P2tog, P7, [Pfb] 4 times, P to last 2 sts, P2tog. (24 sts)
Row 54 (shaping row) K2tog, K8, [Kfb] 4 times, K to last 2 sts, K2tog. (26 sts)
Row 55 (shaping row) P2tog, P9, [Pfb] 4 times, P to last 2 sts, P2tog. (28 sts)
Row 56 (shaping row) K2tog, K10, [Kfb] 4 times, K to last 2 sts, K2tog. (30 sts)
Row 57 (shaping row) P2tog, P11, [Pfb] 4 times, P to last 2 sts, P2tog. (32 sts)
Row 58 (shaping row) K2tog, K12, [Kfb] 4 times, K to last 2 sts, K2tog. (34 sts)
Row 59 (shaping row) P2tog, P13, [Pfb] 4 times, P to last 2 sts, P2tog. (36 sts)
Beg with a K row, work straight in st st for 9 rows, so ending with a *RS* row.
Cast off p-wise.

To make up
Press pieces lightly on wrong side, following instructions on yarn label.

Head and body
Using blunt-ended yarn needle, matching yarn and mattress stitch for seams throughout, sew seam that runs from gathered end of horse along underside of horse and up marker (marking beginning of underside of neck). Then sew cast-off edge of head to shaped side of neck up to marker, leaving remaining head seam open.
Cut out felt pieces for outer and inner eyes and nostrils, using templates (see page 110). Using two strands of stranded cotton and an embroidery sewing needle, sew each inner eye to center of an outer eye with a French knot. (To further secure inner eye, if desired, work short straight stitches around edge of inner eye).

Using two strands of stranded cotton and an embroidery sewing needle, sew eyes and nostrils to horse with short straight stitches.
Sew remaining head seam, leaving an opening for inserting filling. Insert filling, manipulating it to shape horse as shown. Using long tail end of yarn A at cast-on edge of muzzle, run a gathering stitch around cast-on edge of muzzle, pull tight to gather, and secure with a few stitches.

Legs
Sew seam leg and hoof seam at back of each leg. Then fill hoof with toy filling. If you want a stiffened leg, fold a sheet of A4 paper in half widthwise, then roll tightly along diagonal. Insert roll into leg and down into middle of toy filling in hoof. Lightly insert filling around paper roll along leg. Trim paper flush with top of leg. Then run a gathering stitch around top of leg, pull tight and secure with a few stitches, leaving a long length of yarn to sew leg to body. If desired, bend paper/leg at knee to make leg appear flexible.
Prepare all four legs in same way.
To position forelegs on body, start under horse's head at chin seam and measure 11cm/4¼in along seam to under shoulder – place a pin at this point on seam. With front of hoof facing towards nose and each inner leg 2cm/¾in from either side of pin, overcast stitch each foreleg in place around gathered edge, using matching yarn.
To position hind legs, start level with back of forelegs and measure 7cm/2¾in along body seam – place a pin at this point on seam. Overcast stitch each hind leg in place as for forelegs.

Ears
Working a few stitches to secure, sew

together two points of each knitted
ear triangle that have a long tail end of
yarn – this forms a loop at one side
edge of knitted triangle (free point
of triangle forms tip of ear).
With the inside of each ear facing
outwards and outer edge of ear at
position indicated by markers at top of
head, overcast stitch 'row-end loop'
onto horse, using matching yarn.

Mane

For mane, cut 30cm/12in lengths of
yarn B (mohair). Use six or seven
strands of mohair yarn together for
each tuft of mane. Align group of six
or seven strands, fold them in half,
thread fold through a blunt-ended yarn
needle, and slide needle along to
opposite end of yarn. Beginning
between ears, insert needle in and
out at center of head and as needle
emerges, pass it through loop at folded

end of strands. Pull loop down to top
of head to secure, then slip off needle.
Sew on tufts of mane like this all along
fashioned detail made by decreases
along center of back of head. Work
more tufts in this way at either side
this line of tufts, if you wish, to achieve
a full head of hair. If you wanted to use
thicker yarn, use one strand at a time,
double it, thread the loop through the
needle, and make tufts in same way
(see above).

Tail

For tail, cut 60cm/24in lengths of yarn B
(mohair). Sew on tufts of yarn as for
mane, starting at center of tail at the
back end of horse and adding more
tufts around first tuft in circles until tail
has desired fullness.

enchanted land

Princess

Long, long hair, a gown embroidered with pink roses, golden slippers, and a golden crown make this princess a sure favorite. Change the hair color to match your own little princess.

Finished size

Completed toy measures approximately 45cm/17¾in from head to foot.

Yarn

Doll: One 50g/1¾oz ball of Jaeger *Baby Merino 4-Ply* in main color MC (beige/Magnolia 124); *or other 4-ply-weight (US fingering-weight) yarn in skin color of choice*

Hair: One 50g/1¾oz ball of Rowan *All Seasons Cotton* in A (yellow/Citron 216); *or other medium-weight yarn in hair color of choice*

Dress: Small amount of Jaeger *Baby Merino 4-Ply* in B (tangerine/Marigold 096), and one 50g/1¾oz ball each in C (mid rose pink/Princess 126) and D (lilac/Icing 095); *or other 4-ply-weight (US fingering-weight) yarn in 3 colors of choice*

Apron: One 50g/1¾oz ball of Jaeger *Baby Merino 4-Ply* in E (white/Snowdrop 102); *or other 4-ply-weight (US fingering-weight) yarn in color of choice*

Gold embroidery: Use leftover yarn from crown

Embroidered roses (optional): Small amount of Jaeger *Baby Merino 4-Ply* in F (dark rose pink/Red Cheek 094) and C (mid rose pink – see dress yarn); *or other 4-ply-weight (US fingering-weight) yarn in 2 colors of choice*

Crown: Small amount of Rowan *Lurex Shimmer* in G (gold/Antique White Gold 332); *or other lightweight gold metallic yarn*

Slippers: Scrap of a green yarn for leaves, and yarns D and G

Fabric and extras

Felt: Scraps of felt – white for outer eyes, blue for inner eyes, and light pink for mouth

Embroidery thread: Stranded cotton – black for eyes and light pink for mouth and nose

Filling: Polyester toy filling

Needles

Pair of 2¾mm (US size 2) knitting needles
Blunt-ended yarn sewing needle
Embroidery sewing needle

Tension/gauge

30 sts and 38 rows to 10cm/4in measured over st st using 2¾mm (US size 2) needles and yarn MC.

Making the **Princess**

PRINCESS DOLL

To make doll

Using 2¾mm (US size 2) needles and yarn MC (beige), make front, back, arms, and legs as for Basic Girl Doll on pages 20–22.

To make up

Press front and back of doll lightly on wrong side following instructions on yarn label.

Do NOT press arms and legs.

Sew on eyes, nose, and mouth before stitching knitted pieces together.

Eyes

Make up eyes as for Basic Doll, using two strands of black stranded cotton for French knots and for sewing inner and outer eyes in place.

Mouth and nose

Cut out piece of pink felt for mouth, using template (see page 110). Using two strands of pink stranded cotton and embroidery sewing needle, sew on mouth with tiny running stitches, and then work two straight stitches on top of each other for nose.

Body, head, arms, and legs

Sew together pieces for body and head, and sew on arms and legs as for Basic Doll.

Hair

Using yarn A, make a hairpiece with a center parting and sew to doll as for Basic Doll, cutting very long hair strands (Rapunzel style). For two twists at front of hair, twist together two groups of three strands of yarn A and knot at ends to hold twists, then sew in place at center hair parting. Braid a bunch of hair at center back of head.

DRESS WITH APRON

Skirt

Make skirt in one piece as foll:
Using 2¾mm (US size 2) needles and yarn B (tangerine), cast on 160 sts.
Beg with a K row, work in st st until skirt measures approximately 1.5cm/⅝in from cast-on edge, ending with a WS row.
Next row (RS) *K2, K2tog, rep from * to end. (120 sts)
Break off yarn B and change to yarn C (mid rose pink) and cont straight in st st until skirt measures approximately 19cm/7½in from cast-on edge, ending with a WS row.
Next row (RS) *K1, K2tog, rep from * to end. (80 sts)
Purl 1 row.
Next row *K2tog, rep from * to end. (40 sts) Cast off p-wise.

Bodice back and front (both alike)

Using 2¾mm (US size 2) needles and yarn D (lilac), cast on 60 sts.
Beg with a P row, work in st st for 3 rows, so ending with a WS row.
Next row (waistline) (RS) *K2tog, rep from * to end. (30 sts)
Beg with a P row, work straight in st st for 3 rows, so ending with a WS row.
Next row (RS) K6, K2tog, *K5, K2tog, rep from * to last st, K1. (26 sts)
Beg with a P row, work straight in st st for 3 rows, so ending with a WS row.
Next row (RS) K5, *K2tog, K5, rep from * to end. (23 sts)
Beg with a P row, work straight in st st for 21 rows, so ending with a WS row.
Cast off.

Sleeves (make 2)

Using 2¾mm (US size 2) needles and yarn G (gold metallic), cast on 16 sts.
Knit 1 row.
Break off G and change to yarn D (lilac).
Beg with a P row, work straight in st st for 5 rows, so ending with a WS row.

Shape cuff

Next row (RS) K1, *K2tog, K1, rep from * to end. (11 sts)
Next row P1, *P2tog, rep from * to end. (6 sts)
Next row K into front and back of st to inc one st—called *Kfb*—, rep from * to end (to inc into every st). (12 sts)
Next row *P1, P into front and back of st to inc one st—called *Pfb*—, rep from * to end. (18 sts)
Beg with a K row, work straight in st st for 14 rows, so ending with a WS row.

Shape shoulder

Next row (RS) *K2tog, rep from * to end. (9 sts)
Beg with a P row, work straight in st st for 5 rows, so ending with a WS row.
Next row (RS) *K2tog, K to last 2 sts, K2tog. (7 sts)
Break off yarn, thread through rem 7 sts and pull up to gather loosely.

Apron

Using 2¾mm (US size 2) needles and yarn E (white), cast on 80 sts.
Beg with a K row, work in st st until apron measures 17.5cm/7in from cast-on edge, ending with a WS row.
Next row (RS) *K2, K2tog, rep from * to end. (60 sts)
Purl 1 row.
Next row *K1, K2tog, rep from * to end. (40 sts)
Purl 1 row.
Next row *K2tog, rep from * to end. (20 sts)
Next row P2tog, P to last 2 sts, P2tog. (18 sts)

Beg with a K row, work straight in st st for 4 rows, so ending with a WS row. Cast off.

Apron ties (make 2)

Using 2¾mm (US size 2) needles and yarn E (white), cast on 25 sts.
Cast off.

To make up

Press skirt, bodice pieces, bodice sleeves and apron lightly on wrong side following instructions on yarn label. Sew bodice side seams, leaving 12mm/½in from neck edge unsewn to form armholes. Sew sleeve seams, leaving 12mm/½in from neck edge unsewn. Ease each gathered edge of sleeve to fit neck edge to give an off-the-shoulder effect and sew free row-ends at top of sleeve to armholes. Sew back seam on skirt. Slip stitch top of skirt to wrong side of bodice waistline.
Sew cast-off edge of each apron tie to one side of top of apron.

Gold filigree embroidery

Using yarn G (gold metallic) and a blunt-ended yarn needle, embroider the bodice and apron with curlicues as follows:

1 Mark the filigree design on the bodice with pins and then basting stitches. Then using pins, mark four equally spaced points along bottom of the apron about 1cm/½in from cast-on edge. Starting at these points and ending at waist, mark four apron curlicues with basting stitches.

2 To start each curlicue, secure a length of yarn to the wrong side of the knitting and bring it through to the right side at the beginning of the line. Remove the needle.

A child's wishes amount to many and can be somewhat impossible. However, these dolls are highly achievable and can be completed within a week – that's one sorted!

Making the **Princess**

3 Thread a new length of yarn onto the needle and secure it to the wrong side of the knitting.

4 Lay the first length of yarn along the curlicue line and use the second length to secure it in place with small couching stitches worked about 6mm/¼in apart all along the curlicue.

5 At the end of each line, take both yarns back to the wrong side and secure. Remove basting.

Embroidered roses

As an optional extra work four embroidered roses along the bottom of the skirt, one at the beginning of each curlicue, and one rose on the front of the bodice at the shoulder.

This technique may seem a little daunting, but once mastered it is as easy as basic knitting – in fact, the technique is similar to casting on. It is a good idea to practice your first rose on a tension/gauge square.

Using yarns F (dark rose pink) and C (mid rose pink) and a blunt-ended yarn needle, work each cast-on rose as follows:

1 Secure a length of yarn F (dark rose pink) to the back at the position for the center of the rose.

2 Bring the needle to the front and take a tiny backstitch from right to left close to where the needle first emerged, leaving the needle in the fabric.

3 Keeping the thread taut, use your left forefinger to cast on loops onto the tip of the needle – just like the simplest knitting cast-on technique. (The loops once made are identical to close buttonhole stitches). Cast on 12 loops in total, sliding each one down the needle close to the fabric.

4 Holding the cast-on loops in your left hand, pull the needle and thread (with your right hand) through the loops.

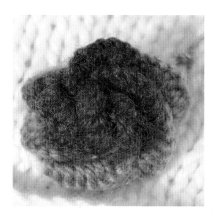

5   To anchor the loops, insert the
    needle through the fabric close to
    where it last emerged and pull the
    thread through. Pull firmly but do not
    let the cast-on loops disappear into
    the knitting. This completes the first
    petal.

6   Work five more inner petals
    spiralling around the center of the
    rose. Make each of these as for the
    first petal, but make the backstitch
    twice as long and cast on 14 loops
    instead of 12.

7   Change to yarn C (mid rose pink)
    and work six more petals around
    and overlapping the inner petals,
    each with 16 loops. This completes
    the rose.

PRINCESS CROWN

To make the crown

Using 2¾mm (US size 2) needles and
yarn G (gold metallic), cast on 8 sts.
Row 1 Cast off first 4 sts k-wise and
slip st on right needle back onto left
needle. (4 sts)
Row 2 Cast on 8 sts next to 4 sts
already on needle, then cast off first 4
sts and slip st on right needle back onto
left needle. (8 sts)

Rep last row 7 times more. (36 sts)
Next row Cast on 1 st next to sts
already on needle, then K all sts to end.
Knit 1 row more.
Cast off k-wise.
Sew crown to top of doll's head in hair.

PRINCESS SLIPPERS

Uppers (make 2)

Beg at toe end, work upper as foll:
Using 2¾mm (US size 2) needles and
yarn G (gold metallic), cast on 3 sts.
Row 1 K to end.
Row 2 *Kfb, rep from * to end. (6 sts)
Rep last 2 rows once more. (12 sts)
Work 5 rows more in garter st (knit
every row).
Cast off k-wise.

Soles (make 2)

Using 2¾mm (US size 2) needles and
yarn D (lilac), cast on 8 sts.
Beg with a K row, work 14 rows in st
st, so ending with a WS row.
Cast off.

To make up

Press each sole flat (be sure to follow
instructions on yarn label for pressing).
Fold each sole in half lengthwise, with

purl-stitch side facing out, and overcast
stitch two side edges of sole together,
stitching across the cast-on edge (toe
end of slipper) and cast-off edge as well.
Shape upper over tip of your index
finger, then lay it over toe-end of slipper,
with sole seam at bottom of slipper.
Sew upper in place, using yarn G.
Embroider a rose on top of each slipper,
working five bullion knots in yarn F
(dark rose pink). Make a loop of green
yarn on each side of rose for leaves.

Castle

It had to be pink with roses around the castle gate. Listen to her desires and follow the basic pattern to create a totally dream-inspiring toy and bedtime comforter.

Finished size

Completed toy measures approximately 30cm/12in wide x 25cm/10in tall, including turrets.

Yarn

Castle: Two 50g/1¾oz balls of Rowan *Handknit Cotton* in main color MC (pink/Shell 310) and one ball in A (light brown/taupe 253); *or other DK-weight (US light-worsted-weight) yarn in 2 colors of choice*

Turret roofs: One 50g/1¾oz ball of Jaeger *Baby Merino 4-Ply* in B (light mauve/Icing 095) used double; *or other 4-ply-weight (US fingering-weight) yarn in color of choice*

Battlement: One 50g/1¾oz ball of Rowan *Handknit Cotton* in C (light grey/Chime 204); *or other DK-weight (US light-worsted-weight) yarn in color of choice*

Picot edging and turret trim: Small amount of Rowan *Handknit Cotton* in D (off-white/Ecru 251); *or other DK-weight (US light-worsted-weight) yarn in color of choice*

Door, window, and drawbridge: Small amount of Rowan *4-Ply Soft* in E (dark brown/Express 389) used double; *or other 4-ply-weight (US fingering-weight) yarn in color of choice*

Fabric and extras

Embroidery thread: Scraps of wool 4-ply-weight yarn (US fingering-weight) – or stranded cotton or pearl embroidery thread – for embroidery, in turquoise, light mauve, mid rose pink, sage green, red, pale rose pink, white, and yellow; plus a scrap of wool tapestry yarn in light apple green for stems, and a scrap of lightweight gold metallic yarn for drawbridge chain and embroidery on lower window

Felt: 20cm/8in x 10cm/4in piece of felt in light brown or light grey for castle base

Filling: Polyester toy filling

Making the **Castle**

Needles and hook

Pair of 3¼mm (US size 3) knitting needles
4.00mm (US size F/5) crochet hook
Blunt-ended yarn sewing needle

Tension/gauge

28 sts and 36 rows to 10cm/4in measured over st st using 3¼mm (US size 3) needles and yarn MC.

Special yarn note

Be sure to use yarns C and D double – these are 4-ply-weight (US fingering-weight) yarns. If you are buying a different yarn, you can use a single strand of a double-knitting-weight (US light-worsted-weight) yarn instead.

Castle front

Castle is worked starting with basketweave wall at base.
Using 3¼mm (US size 3) needles and

yarn A (light brown), cast on 40 sts.
Beg basketweave patt as foll:
Patt row 1 (WS) K1, P to last st, K1.
Patt row 2 Rep row 1.
Patt row 3 K3, *P4, K2, rep from * to last st, K1.
Patt row 4 K1, *P2, K4, rep from * to last 3 sts, P2, K1.
Patt row 5 Rep row 3.
Patt row 6 Rep row 1.
Patt row 7 K1, P3, *K2, P4, rep from * to last 6 sts, K2, P3, K1.

Patt row 8 K4, *P2, K4, rep from * to end.

Patt row 9 Rep row 7.

Patt rows 10–13 Rep rows 2–5.

This completes castle wall.

Break off yarn A and change to yarn MC (pink).

Beg with a K row, work in st st for 24 rows.

Cast off.

Castle back

Work exactly as for front.

Castle roof

Oval roof top fits on top of castle like a lid.

Using 3¼mm (US size 3) needles and yarn MC (pink), cast on 80 sts.

Row 1 *K8, K2tog, rep from * to end. (72 sts)

Row 2 *P7, P2tog, rep from * to end. (64 sts)

Row 3 *K6, K2tog, rep from * to end. (56 sts)

Row 4 *P5, P2tog, rep from * to end. (48 sts)

Row 5 *K4, K2tog, rep from * to end. (40 sts)

Row 6 *P3, P2tog, rep from * to end. (32 sts)

Row 7 *K2, K2tog, rep from * to end. (24 sts)

Row 8 *P1, P2tog, rep from * to end. (16 sts)

Row 9 *K2tog, rep from * to end. (8 sts)

Break off yarn leaving a long tail-end, then thread yarn end onto a blunt-ended yarn needle and pass yarn needle through 8 sts as they are slipped off knitting needle. Pull tight to gather and secure with a few sts.

Turrets (make 2)

Using 3¼mm (US size 3) needles and yarn MC (pink), cast on 36 sts.

Beg with a K row, work 14 rows in st st, so ending with a WS row.

Shape top

Next row (dec row) (RS) *K2, K2tog, rep from * to end. (27 sts)

Purl 1 row.

Next row (dec row) *K1, K2tog, rep from * to end. (18 sts)

Purl 1 row.

Next row (dec row) *K2tog, rep from * to end. (9 sts)

Purl 1 row.

Break off yarn leaving a long tail-end, then thread yarn end onto a blunt-ended yarn needle and pass yarn needle through 9 sts as they are slipped off knitting needle. Pull tight to gather sts and secure.

Turret roofs (make 2)

Using 3¼mm (US size 3) needles and 2 strands of yarn B (light mauve) held tog, cast on 30 sts. (Use yarn B double throughout.)

Row 1 P to end.

Row 2 (RS) *K1, K into front and back of next st to inc one st—called *Kfb*—, rep from * to end. (45 sts)

Beg with a P row, work straight in st st for 3 rows, so ending with a WS row.

Shape top

Next row (dec row) (RS) *K3, K2tog, rep from * to end. (36 sts)

Beg with a P row, work straight in st st for 3 rows, so ending with a WS row.

Next row (dec row) (RS) *K2, K2tog, rep from * to end. (27 sts)

Beg with a P row, work straight in st st for 3 rows, so ending with a WS row.

Next row (dec row) (RS) *K1, K2tog, rep from * to end. (18 sts)

Beg with a P row, work straight in st st for 3 rows, so ending with a WS row.

Next row (dec row) (RS) *K2tog, rep from * to end. (9 sts)

Break off yarn leaving a long tail-end, then thread yarn end onto a blunt-ended yarn needle and pass yarn needle through 9 sts as they are slipped off knitting needle. Pull tight to gather sts and secure.

Battlement

Battlement is worked in one piece.

Using 3¼mm (US size 3) needles and yarn C (light grey), cast on 7 sts.

Work 8 rows in garter st (knit every row).

Cont in garter st, beg patt as foll:

****Next row** Cast on 5 sts next to 7 sts already on needle, then K all sts. (12 sts)

Work straight in garter st for 5 rows.***

Next row Cast off 5 sts, K to end. (7 sts)

Work straight in garter st for 5 rows.**

Rep from ** to ** until piece fits along cast-off edges of castle front and back, ending at ***. Cast off k-wise.

Picot edging for battlement

Using 3 ¼mm (US size 3) needles and yarn D (off-white), cast on 6 sts.

Row 1 Cast off first 3 sts k-wise and slip st on right needle back onto left needle. (3 sts)

Row 2 Cast on 6 sts next to 3 sts already on needle, then cast off first 3 sts k-wise and slip st on right needle back onto left needle. (6 sts)

Rep last row until edging is same length as battlement.

Work 2 rows in garter st. Cast off k-wise.

Door

Using 3¼mm (US size 3) needles and 2 strands of yarn E (dark brown) held tog,

Making the **Castle**

cast on 12 sts. (Use yarn E double throughout.)

Rib row 1 K1, [P2, K2] twice, P2, K1.

Rib row 2 P1, [K2, P2] twice, K2, P1.

Last 2 rows form rib patt.

Work 16 rows more in rib.

Next row (dec row) P2tog, P1, K2, P2, K2, P1, P2tog. (10 sts)

Next row (dec row) K2tog, P2, K2, P2, K2tog. (8 sts)

Next row (dec row) K2tog, K1, P2, K1, K2tog. (6 sts)

Next row (dec row) P2tog, K2, P2tog. (4 sts)

Cast off in rib.

Drawbridge

Using 3¼mm (US size 3) needles and 2 strands of yarn E (dark brown) held tog, cast on 15 sts. (Use yarn E double throughout.)

Work in garter st (knit every row) until row-end edge of drawbridge fits across width of door. Cast off k-wise.

Windows (make 3)

Using 3¼mm (US size 3) needles and 2 strands of yarn E (dark brown) held tog, cast on 8 sts. (Use yarn E double throughout.)

Beg with a K row, work 6 rows in st st, so ending with a WS row.

Next row (dec row) (RS) K2tog, K4, K2tog. (6 sts)

Next row (dec row) P2tog, P2, P2tog. (4 sts)

Next row (dec row) [K2tog] twice. (2 sts)

Purl 1 row. Cast off.

Picot edging for window

Make a picot edging to fit across bottom of one window, working as for picot edging for battlement.

To make up

Press pieces lightly on wrong side, following instructions on yarn label and avoiding garter stitch, basketweave pattern and ribbing.

Use a blunt-ended yarn needle for all seams and embroidery on castle. Use matching yarn for all seams and specified yarn for embroidery.

Door and drawbridge

Using two strands of turquoise 4-ply yarn, embroider a French knot on door for doorknocker.

Pin door to middle of castle front, aligning cast-on edges. Using two strands of light mauve 4-ply yarn, blanket stitch door to castle along edge of door. Overcast stitch a row-end edge of drawbridge to lower edge of door, using yarn E (dark brown).

Using gold metallic yarn, make two twisted cords for drawbridge chains, and sew in place as shown.

Windows

Using one strand of mid rose pink 4-ply yarn, work a vertical and a horizontal backstitch line across center of two windows. Work lines on third window in same way, using gold metallic yarn; then sew picot edging to bottom cast-on edge of this window.

Using two strands of light mauve 4-ply yarn, blanket stitch window with gold lines to left of door. Sew one of each of remaining windows to each turret piece in same way.

Floral embroidery

At each side of door, couch in place a trail of green stems, using one strand of light apple green tapestry wool on one side and one strand of sage green 4-ply yarn on the other side (see page 46 for how to work couching).

With one strand of 4-ply yarn in red, pale rose pink or mid rose pink yarn, work roses along green stems, varying sizes by working more or fewer outer petals (see page 34 for how to work roses).

Using one strand of white 4-ply yarn, work flowers in lazy daisy stitch around door work. Add lazy daisy stitch leaves around white flowers, using one strand of turquoise 4-ply yarn for some and one strand of sage green 4-ply yarn for others. Work a French knot at center of each white flower, using one strand of yellow 4-ply yarn.

If desired, add similar floral embroidery to castle back.

Castle assembly

With right sides together, sew back of castle to front along sides, using backstitch. Turn right side out.

Overcast stitch oval roof ('lid') to cast-off edge of top of castle.

Turn castle upside down and firmly fill with toy filling. Trim off corners on felt for base of castle to form an oval shape. Pin felt base to cast-on edge of castle wall, making sure drawbridge is outside. Then overcast stitch base in place.

Overcast stitch battlement to upper edge of castle, then sew on picot edging.

Turrets

With right sides together, sew row-end edges of each turret together and turn right side out. Fill turrets with toy filling, making them round.

With right sides together, sew row-end edges of each turret roof together and turn right side out. Fill roofs, manipulating toy filling to form tapered shape.

Overcast stitch each roof to a turret.

Next, work decorative edging for base of each turret roof. Using 4.00mm (US size F/5) crochet hook and yarn D (off-white), work a length of chain long enough to fit around circumference of turret. Fasten off.

Make a second length in same way for other turret and sew one length to each turret.

Overcast stitch turrets with their roofs to roof of castle, one near each outside edge.

fairy dream

Fairy

This ethereal lady and her accompanying baby, both with whispy pink hair, are the epitome of delicate garden fairies. To change their look completely, just change the eye and hair colors.

Finished size

Completed Fairy measures approximately 45cm/17¾in from head to foot and Baby Fairy approximately 28cm/11in.

Yarn

Dolls: One 50g/1¾oz ball of Rowan *RYC Cashcotton 4-Ply* in main color MC (light pink/Sugar 901); *or other 4-ply-weight (US fingering-weight) yarn in skin color of choice*

Hair: One 25g/1oz ball of Rowan *Kidsilk Haze* in A (pink/Grace 580); *or other lightweight mohair in hair color of choice*

Fairy's dress: 50g/1¾oz ball of Rowan *All Seasons Cotton* in B (light green/Lime Leaf 217); *or other medium-weight yarn in color of choice*

Petals of Fairy's corsage: Small amount of Jaeger *Baby Merino 4-Ply* in C (white/Snowdrop 102); *or other 4-ply-weight (US fingering-weight) yarn in color of choice*

Center of Fairy's corsage: Small amount of Rowan *4-Ply Cotton* in D (orange/Tutti Frutti 138); *or other 4-ply-weight (US fingering-weight) yarn in color of choice*

Baby Fairy's pants and socks: Use leftover yarn C (white)

Fabric and extras

Felt: Scraps of felt – white for outer eyes and wings, brown for inner eye and wing motifs, light pink for mouths and wing motifs, and hot pink and yellow for wing motifs

Embroidery thread: Stranded cotton – black for eyes, light pink for mouths, and mid rose pink for wings

Sewing thread: Matching sewing threads, for sewing motifs on fairy wings and securing filigree

Filling: Polyester toy filling

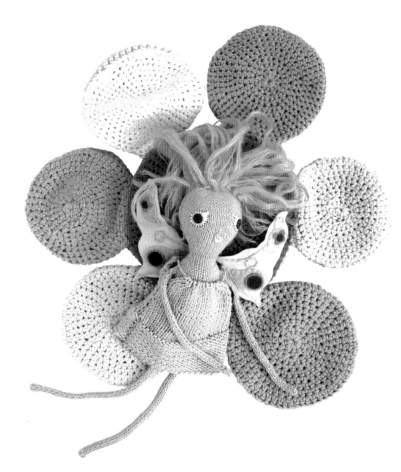

Making the **Fairy**

Needles

Dolls: Pair of 2¾mm (US size 2) knitting needles

Fairy's Dress: Pair of 4½mm (US size 7) knitting needles

Blunt-ended yarn sewing needle

Embroidery sewing needle

Tension/gauge

Dolls: 30 sts and 38 rows to 10cm/4in measured over st st using 2¾mm (US size 2) needles and yarn MC.

Fairy's Dress: 16 sts and 23 rows to 10cm/4in measured over st st using 4½mm (US size 7) needles and yarn B.

FAIRY DOLL

To make doll

Using 2¾mm (US 2) needles and yarn MC (light pink), make front, back, arms, and legs as for Basic Girl Doll on pages 20–22.

To make up

Press front and back of doll lightly on wrong side following instructions on yarn label. Do NOT press arms and legs. Sew on eyes, nose, and mouth, then make wings before stitching knitted pieces together.

Eyes

Make and sew on eyes as for Basic Doll, using two strands of black stranded cotton for French knot and for sewing inner and outer eyes in place.

Mouth and nose

Cut out piece of pink felt for mouth, using template (see page 110). Using two strands of pink stranded cotton and embroidery sewing needle, sew on mouth with tiny running stitches and work two straight stitches on top of each other for nose.

Body, head, arms, and legs

Sew together pieces for body and head, and sew on arms and legs as for Basic Doll, but prepare wings beforehand (see below). Catch each wing in at neck seam.

Hair

For hair, cut 70cm/28in lengths of yarn A (mohair). Sew on hair in tufts as for Basic Doll.

Fairy wings

1 Using the templates for Fairy wings (see page 112), cut out the wings from the white felt and the motifs from the brown, hot pink, and light pink felt. Place the motifs on one side of the wings and when you are happy with the placements, stitch the shapes in place with tiny running stitches, using an embroidery sewing needle and matching thread.

2 Carefully mark the filigree design on each of the wings with basting stitches.

3 To start each line of filigree, use an embroidery sewing needle to secure a length of yarn MC to the wrong side of the wing and bring it through to the right side at the beginning of the line. Remove the needle.

4 Thread the embroidery sewing needle with a matching sewing thread and secure the thread to the wrong side of the wing.

5 Lay the length of yarn along the basted guideline and use the sewing thread to secure it in place with small couching stitches worked about 6mm/¼in apart all along the filigree line.

6 At the end of each line, take the yarn and the thread back to the wrong side and secure.

FAIRY'S DRESS

Back

Using 4½mm (US size 7) needles and yarn B (light green), cast on 25 sts. Work 3 rows in garter st (knit every row). Beg with a P row, work in rev st st for 12 rows, so ending with a WS (K) row.

Shape skirt

Change to st st and cont as foll:

Next row (RS) [K7, K2tog] twice, K7. (23 sts)

Beg with a P row, work straight in st st for 3 rows, so ending with a WS row.

Next row (RS) K7, K2tog, K5, K2tog, K7. (21 sts)

Beg with a P row, work straight in st st for 7 rows, so ending with a WS row.

Next row (RS) K6, K into front and back of next st—called *Kfb*—, K6, Kfb, K7. (23 sts)

Beg with a P row, work straight in st st for 5 rows, so ending with a WS row.

Shape armholes

Cont in st st throughout, cast off 2 sts at beg of each of next 2 rows. (19 sts)

Next row (RS) K2, K2tog, K to last 4 sts, K2tog, K2. (17 sts)

Next row P2, P2tog, P to last 2 sts, P2tog, P2. (15 sts)

Next row K2, K2tog, K to last 4 sts, K2tog, K2. (13 sts)

Break off yarn, leaving a long tail-end, then thread yarn end onto a blunt-ended yarn needle and pass yarn needle through sts as they are slipped off knitting needle. Pull yarn to loosely gather top of back and leave long end to use for making straps.

Front

Work exactly as for back, but leave rem 13 stitches on needle. Then take long tail-end at top of back (that was used

to gather back sts) and thread it through 13 front sts as they are slipped off knitting needle. Pull loosely to gather and leave a strand between back and front for one strap. Make second strap by securing yarn to back.

To make up

Press back and front lightly on WS following instructions on yarn label. Sew back and front together along side seams.

FAIRY'S CORSAGE

Flower petals

Using 2¾mm (US size 2) needles and yarn C (white), cast on 10 sts.
Row 1 Cast off 6 sts k-wise, K to end. (4 sts)
Row 2 K4.
Row 3 Cast on 6 sts next to sts already on needle, then cast off same 6 sts k-wise, K to end. (4sts)
Rep rows 2 and 3 eleven times more. Cast off.

Flower center

Using 2¾mm (US size 2) needles and yarn D (orange), cast on 5 sts.
Work 5 rows in garter st (knit every row). Holding needle with sts in right hand, use left needle to pick up 2nd st on right needle and slip it over first st and off needle, then slip 3rd st on right needle over first and off needle, slip 4th and 5th sts over first and off needle in same way. Fasten off, leaving a long tail-end of yarn.
Using tail-end of yarn and a blunt-ended yarn needle, work running stitch around outside edge of flower center. Pull tight to gather edge, then sew to center of flower. Attach corsage to front of head.

BABY FAIRY DOLL

Front

Front of doll body and head are worked in one piece, as foll:

Body

Using 2¾mm (US size 2) needles and yarn MC (skin color), cast on 13 sts.
Place *marker* on 3rd and 9th cast-on sts to mark outside thigh position for each leg.
Beg with a K row, work 22 rows in st st, so ending with a WS row.
Shape shoulders and neck
Next row (RS) K2tog, K to last 2 sts, K2tog. (11 sts)
Next row P2tog, P to last 2 sts, P2tog. (9 sts)
Place *marker* at each end of last row for underarm positions.
Rep last 2 rows once more. (5 sts)
Beg with a K row, work straight in st st for 3 rows, so ending with a *RS* row.
Shape head
Next row (WS) Cast on 1 st, P to last st, P into front and back of st to inc one st—called *Pfb.* (7 sts)
Next row Cast on 1 st, K to last st, K into front and back of st to inc one st—called *Kfb.* (9 sts)
Rep last 2 rows 3 times more, so ending with a *RS* row. (21 sts)
Beg with a P row, work straight in st st for 15 rows, so ending with a WS row.
Next row (RS) *K2tog, rep from * to last st, K1. (11 sts)
Purl 1 row.
Next row *K2tog, rep from * to last st, K1. (6 sts).
Cast off.

Back

Make exactly as for front.

Arms (make 2)

Using 2¾mm (US size 2) needles and yarn MC, cast on 3 sts.
Beg with a K row, work in st st until arm measures 8cm/3½in from cast-on edge, ending with a WS row.
Cast off.
(Arms curl into tubes naturally and do not need seaming).

Legs (make 2)

Using 2¾mm (US size 2) needles and yarn C (white), cast on 4 sts.
Beg with a K row, work in st st until 'sock' measures 7cm/2¾in.
Break off yarn C and change to yarn MC (skin color).
Cont in st st until leg measures 16cm/6¼in from cast-on edge, ending with a WS row.
Cast off.
(Legs curl into tubes naturally and do not need seaming).

To make up

Press front and back of doll lightly on wrong side following instructions on yarn label. Do NOT press arms and legs. Before sewing the doll pieces together, make wings as for Fairy (see page 46), but using white and yellow felt and Baby Fairy templates, omitting filigree embroidery, and stitching a French knot at center of each motif using 2 strands of mid rose pink stranded cotton.
Eyes, mouth, and nose
Work eyes, nose, and mouth as for Fairy.
Body and head
With right sides together and using a blunt-ended yarn needle and matching yarn, sew back of doll to front with backstitches, catching in wings at neck and leaving an opening at bottom edge

for turning right side out.

Turn right side out and lightly fill doll with toy filling.

Overcast stitch opening closed.

Arms

Weave in cast-on and cast-off yarn ends on each arm to neaten. Sew cast-on edge of each arm to body at an underarm marker, with row ends curled in on underside of arm.

Legs

Weave in cast-on and cast-off yarn ends on each leg to neaten. Sew cast-off edge of each leg to body at a leg marker, with row ends curled in towards back.

Hair

For hair, cut 22–50cm/8¾–20in lengths of yarn A (mohair) and attach in tufts as for Fairy.

BABY FAIRY'S PANTS

Back and front (both alike)

Using 2¾mm (US size 2) needles and yarn C (white), cast on 4 sts.

Beg with a K row, work 2 rows in st st, so ending with a WS row.

Next row Kfb, K to last st, Kfb. (6 sts)

Purl 1 row.

Rep last 2 rows 4 times more, so ending with a WS row. (14 sts)

Picot edging

Next row (RS) Cast off 3 sts k-wise, *slip st on right needle back onto left needle, cast on 1 st next to sts on left needle, cast off 3 sts k-wise, rep from * to end. Fasten off.

To make up

Press back and front lightly on wrong side following instructions on yarn label. Sew cast-on edges of back and front together for crotch seam. Sew side seams.

Flower

Crocheted in an extremely soft cashmere-blend yarn, this flower is a totally cuddly and unputdownable item. First a bed for the fairies, then a pillow, then a loveable comforter.

Finished size
Completed flower toy measures approximately 56cm/22in in diameter.

Yarn
Small amounts of 11 colors as follows – Rowan *RYC Cashsoft Baby DK* in 5 colors (pale yellow/Limone 802, pale green/Lime 509, white/Snowman 800, baby blue/Ballad Blue 508, and golden yellow/Clementine 510); Rowan *RYC Cashcotton DK* in 3 colors (orange/Geranium 604, turquoise/Pool 602, and pale blue/Cool 601); and Rowan *Wool Cotton* in 3 colors (pink/Flower 943, pale purple/Violet 943, and peach/Mellow Yellow 942) – *or other DK-weight (US light-worsted-weight) yarn in 11 colors of choice*

Extras
Thread: Neutral colored sewing thread for sewing circles together
Filling: Polyester toy filling

Hook and needles
5.00mm (US size H/8) crochet hook
Sewing needle (or sewing machine)
Blunt-ended yarn sewing needle

Tension
15 sts and 14½ rows to 10cm/4in measured over double crochet/US single crochet and using a 5.00mm (US size H/8) hook (however working to exact tension is not essential).

Flower center (make 2)
Note: (dc) = US single crochet (sc)
Using 5.00mm (US size H/8) hook and yarn color of choice, and leaving a long tail-end of yarn (for pulling central hole closed afterwards), make 6ch and join with a ss into first ch to form a ring.
Round 1 (RS) 1ch, 12dc into ring, working over tail of yarn. Do not turn at end of rounds, but work with RS always facing.
Round 2 1dc into each of 12dc of previous round. (12dc)
Round 3 2dc into each dc to end. (24dc)
Round 4 1dc into each dc to end. (24dc)
Round 5 1dc into first dc, 2dc into next dc, *1dc into next dc, 2dc into next dc, rep from * to end. (36dc)
Rounds 6 and 7 Rep round 4 twice.
Round 8 1dc into each of first 2dc, 2dc into next dc, *1dc into each of next 2dc, 2dc into next dc, rep from * to end. (48dc)**
Rounds 9 and 10 Rep round 4 twice.
Round 11 1dc into each of first 3dc, 2dc into next dc, *1dc into each of next 3dc, 2dc into next dc, rep from * to end. (60dc)

Rounds 12 and 13 Rep round 4 twice.
Round 14 1dc into each of first 4dc, 2dc into next dc, *1dc into each of next 4dc, 2dc into next dc, rep from * to the end. (72dc)
Rounds 15 and 16 Rep round 4 twice. Cont in dc in this way, working 12 evenly spaced increases on next round and then every foll 3rd round until circle measures 24cm/9½in in diameter, ending with an inc round.
Work 1ss into next stitch and fasten off. Work another circle in same way, but using yarn in a contrasting color.

Petals (make 12)
Work as for flower center to **, but using yarn color of choice.
Next round 1dc into each dc to end. Work 1 ss into next stitch and fasten off. Work 11 more circles in same way, but using a different color yarn for each one.

To make up
Pull long tail-end of yarn at center of each circle to tighten up hole and weave it in on wrong side. Weave in all remaining loose ends.
Press each circle lightly *on right side of double crochet* following instructions on yarn label.
Pin two large flower center circles together, with *wrong sides of double*

Making the **Flower**

Young children derive much pleasure from tucking up toys in covers and blankets. This flower is a soft cushion with petals to lay over the sleepy fairies. Make extra crochet blankets to complete a flower bed set.

crochet facing each other and lining up stitches along outside edge (wrong side of double crochet texture is used for outside of flower).

Using sewing needle or sewing machine, backstitch circles together close to edge, leaving an opening to turn right side out.

Turn right side out and lightly fill flower center with toy filling. Finish seam to close opening.

Join pairs of petal circles together in same way, using two contrasting colors for each petal.

Arrange prepared petals around flower center and pin in place. Using a blunt-ended yarn needle and a matching yarn, sew each petal to flower center by overcast stitching along 6dc of each circle.

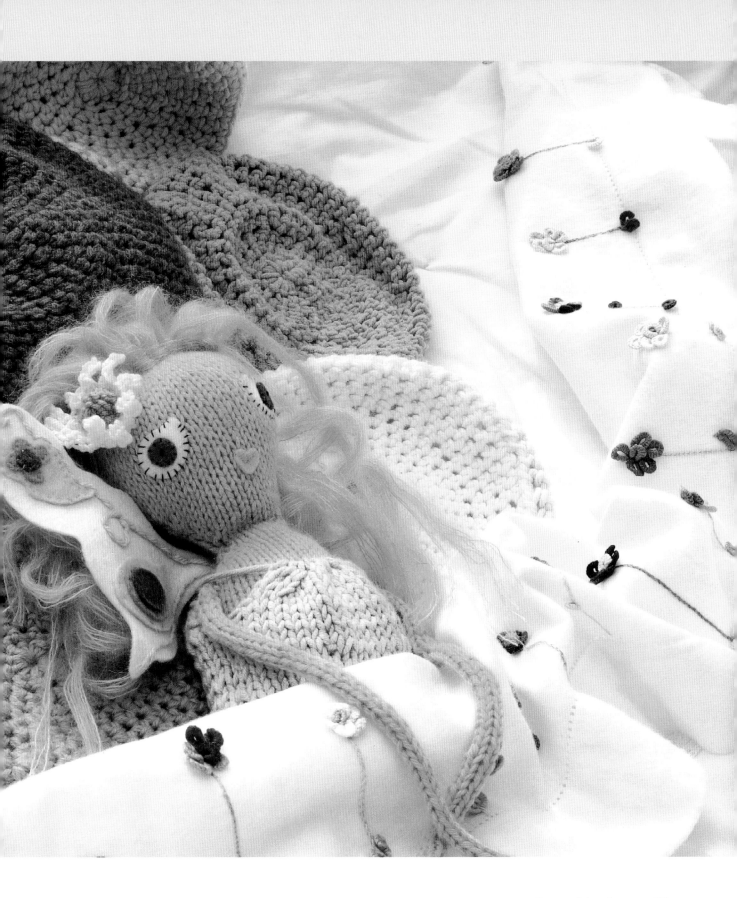

Unicorn

This dreamily enchanting toy is knit in a baby-soft yarn. She's an absolute hit with the little girls, especially since she stands up like a baby foal, thanks to rolled up paper inserted in the legs.

Finished size

Completed toy measures approximately 40cm/15¾in long x 36cm/14¼in tall.

Yarn

Unicorn: Four 50g/1¾oz balls of Rowan *RYC Cashsoft Baby DK* in main color MC (white/Snowman 800); *or other DK-weight (US light-worsted-weight) yarn in color of choice*

Muzzle and hooves: One 50g/1¾oz ball of Rowan *RYC Cashsoft Baby DK* in A (light brown/Crocus 808); *or other DK-weight (US light-worsted-weight) yarn in color of choice*

Mane and tail: 25g/1oz ball of Rowan *Kidsilk Night* in B (off-white/Starlight 607); *or other lightweight mohair in color of choice*

Horn: Small amount of Rowan *Lurex Shimmer* in C (gold/Antique White Gold 332) *or other lightweight gold metallic yarn*; and scrap of 4-ply-weight (US fingering-weight) yarn in D (white)

Blanket: Small amount of Rowan *RYC Cashcotton DK* in E (pale blue/Blue Boy 809); *or other DK-weight (US light-worsted-weight) yarn in color of choice*

Blanket flowers: Rowan yarns as follows – *RYC Cashcotton DK* in white (White 600) and orange (Geranium 604); *Handknit Cotton* in grey-blue (Nautical 311), green (Slippery 316), mid

yellow (Buttercup 320), hot pink (Slick 313), and pale pink (Shell 310); *Cotton Rope* in light yellow (Lemonade/060); *RYC Baby Cashsoft DK* in pale yellow (Limone 802); *All Seasons Cotton* in mid blue (Symphony 187); and *4-Ply Soft* in dark orange (Sandalwood 392)

and magenta (Wink 377); *or other DK-weight (US light-worsted-weight) yarn in white, orange, grey-blue, green, mid yellow, hot pink, pale pink, light yellow, pale yellow, mid blue and a 4-ply-weight (US fingering-weight) yarn in dark orange and magenta*

Making the **Unicorn**

Fabric and extras

Felt: Scraps of felt – cream for outer eyes, sky blue for inner eye, and light pink for nostrils

Embroidery thread: Stranded cotton – black and dark grey for eyes and light pink for nostrils

Filling: Polyester toy filling

Needles and hooks

Pair of 3¾mm (US size 5) knitting needles

Blunt-ended yarn sewing needle

Embroidery sewing needle

3.00mm and 4.00mm (US sizes D/3 and F/5) crochet hooks

Tension/gauge

Unicorn: 22 sts and 30 rows to 10cm/4in measured over st st using 3¾mm (US size 5) needles and yarn MC.

Blanket: Working to a specific tension/gauge is not essential for blanket.

UNICORN

To make toy

Using 3¾mm (US size 5) needles and yarn A (light brown) for muzzle and hooves and yarn MC (white) for Unicorn, make head and body, ears, and legs as for Basic Horse on pages 23–27.

Unicorn horn

Using 3¾mm (US size 5) needles and one strand each of yarn C (gold metallic) and yarn D (white) held tog, cast on 16 sts.

Work horn in rev st st as foll:

Row 1 (RS) P to end.

Row 2 (dec row) K2tog, K to last 2 sts, K2tog. (14 sts)

Rep last 2 rows twice more. (10 sts)

Beg with a P row, work 7 rows in rev st st, so ending with a *RS* (P) row.

Next row (dec row) (WS) K2tog, K to last 2 sts, K2tog. (8 sts)

Purl 1 row.

Rep last 2 rows once more. (6 sts)

Next row (dec row) K2tog, K2, K2tog. (4 sts)

Beg with a P row, work 3 rows in rev st st, so ending with a *RS* (P) row.

Next row (dec row) (WS) [K2tog] twice. (2 sts)

Purl 1 row.

Break off yarn leaving a long tail-end, then thread yarn end onto a blunt-ended yarn needle and pass yarn needle through 2 rem sts as they are slipped off knitting needle. Pull tight to gather sts, leaving long tail-end to sew horn seam.

To make up

Press pieces lightly on wrong side following instructions on yarn label.

Head and body

Sew head and body seams as for Basic Horse, using two strands of black stranded cotton for French knot on eyes, two strands of dark grey for sewing inner and outer eyes in place, and two strands of light pink for sewing nostrils in place.

Horn

Sew horn seam, insert toy filling and slip stitch to head between eyes as shown.

Legs, ears, mane and tail

Prepare and sew on legs, ears, mane, and tail as for Basic Horse.

BLANKET

To make blanket

Note: (dc) = US single crochet (sc); (tr) = US double crochet (dc)

Using 3.00mm (US size D/3) crochet

hook and E (pale blue), make 23ch.

Row 1 1dc into 2nd ch from hook, 1dc into each of rem 21ch. Turn. (22dc)

Row 2 1ch, 1dc into each dc to end. Turn.

Last row forms dc.

Work in dc until blanket measures 27cm/10¾in. Fasten off.

Buttonhole strap

Using 3.00mm (US size D/3) crochet hook and E (pale blue), make 23ch.

Row 1 1dc into 2nd ch from hook, 1dc into each of rem ch. Turn. (22dc)

Row 2 1ch, 1dc into each dc to end, then work 10ch.

Fasten off, leaving a long tail-end of yarn. Sew tail-end of yarn to last dc of last row to form a chain buttonhole loop at end of strap.

Button

Using 3.00mm (US size D/3) crochet hook and white yarn, and leaving a long tail-end of yarn (for pulling central hole closed afterwards), make 6ch and join with a ss into first ch to form a ring.

Round 1 (RS) 1ch, 12dc into ring (working over tail of yarn), 1ss into first dc.

Fasten off.

Pull long tail-end of yarn at center to tighten up hole and use later to sew to blanket.

Circles flower

Circles flower is worked in seven circular pieces – two for flower center and five for petals.

Circle motif for center

Using 3.00mm (US size D/3) crochet hook and orange yarn, and leaving a long tail-end of yarn (for pulling central hole closed afterwards), make 6ch and

Delicate as a baby foal, this unicorn would appeal to all those little girls who dream of stumbling upon a secret fairy world at the bottom of their garden.

join with a ss into first ch to form a ring.

Round 1 (RS) 1ch, 12dc into ring (working over tail of yarn), 1ss into first dc. Do not turn at end of rounds, but work with RS always facing.

Round 2 2dc into same dc as ss was worked, 1dc into each dc to end, 1ss into first dc. (24dc) Fasten off.

Pull long tail-end of yarn at center of flower to tighten up hole and weave in on wrong side.

Circle motifs for petals

For petals, make five circles as for center circle motif, using grey-blue yarn.

Flower center

Using dark orange yarn, work a circle as for button.

Pull long tail-end of yarn at center to tighten up hole and use to sew to center motif.

Using a blunt-ended yarn needle and matching yarn, overcast stitch each of five petals to center motif.

Four-petal flower (make 2)

Using 3.00mm (US size D/3) crochet hook and white yarn, and leaving a long tail-end of yarn (for pulling central hole closed afterwards), make 5ch and join with a ss into first ch to form a ring.

Round 1 (RS) 1ch, 9dc into ring (working over tail of yarn), 1ss into first dc. Do not turn at end of rounds, but work with RS always facing.

Round 2 *3ch, 3tr into next dc, 3ch, 1dc into next dc, rep from * 3 times more, 1ss into first of first 3ch. Fasten off.

Pull long tail-end of yarn at center to tighten up hole and use later to sew to blanket.

Make a second four-petal flower in same way, but using 4.00mm (US size F/5) hook and light yellow yarn. For this second flower, work a center circle as for button, using grey-blue yarn and 3.00mm (US size D/3) hook.

Five-petal flower (make 3)

Using 3.00mm (US size D/3) crochet hook and pale yellow yarn, and leaving a long tail-end of yarn (for pulling central hole closed afterwards), make 8ch and join with a ss into first ch to form a ring.

Round 1 (RS) 1ch, 16dc into ring (working over tail of yarn), 1ss into first dc. Do not turn at end of rounds, but work with RS always facing.

Round 2 4ch, *[2tr into next dc] twice, 3ch, 1dc into next dc, rep from * 4 times more, 1ss into first of first 4ch. Fasten off.

Pull long tail-end of yarn at center to tighten up hole and use later to sew to blanket.

Make a second five-petal flower in same way, but using 4.00mm (US size F/5) hook and green yarn. For this second flower, work a center circle as for circle motif on circles flower, using mid yellow yarn and 3.00mm (US size

D/3) hook.

Make a third five-petal flower in same way, but using 4.00mm (US size F/5) hook and mid blue yarn. For this third flower, work a center circle as for button, using hot pink yarn and 3.00mm (US size D/3) hook.

Scallop flower

Using 3.00mm (US size D/3) crochet hook and magenta yarn, and leaving a long tail-end of yarn (for pulling central hole closed afterwards), make 5ch and join with a ss into first ch to form a ring.

Round 1 (RS) 1ch, 10dc into ring (working over tail of yarn), 1ss into first dc. Do not turn at end of rounds, but work with RS always facing.

Round 2 *3tr into next dc, 1ss into next dc, rep from * 4 times more. Fasten off, leaving a long tail of yarn to sew flower to blanket.

Pull long tail-end of yarn at center to tighten up hole and use later to sew to blanket.

Circle motifs (make 3)

For more pattern on blanket, make three circles.

Using 3.00mm (US size D/3) crochet hook and pale pink yarn, work first circle as for circle motif on circles flower.

Make second circle in same way as first, but using magenta yarn for first round and yarn MC (pale blue) for second round.

Using 3.00mm (US size D/3) crochet hook and white yarn, work third circle as for button.

To make up

Do not press.

Using a blunt-ended yarn needle, sew on button, straps and flowers as foll:

Straps

Sew button to center of foundation-ch end of blanket (if desired work a contrasting colored stitch at center of button). Sew strap to center of other end of blanket.

Flowers and motifs

Sew centers to flowers with contrasting centers, using long tail-ends at centers. Arrange flowers and motifs on blanket, at random. Using matching yarn, overcast stitch circles flower in place. Sew on other flowers and circle motifs, using long tail-end of yarn at center, or attaching with a French knot through center.

Place blanket on Unicorn and button strap in place under Unicorn's belly.

wild trail

Cowboy

An appealing boy's toy with loads of character, this cowboy is a jeaned meany with a cuddly nature! It would be fun to make two – a goody and a baddy – for that sundown shoot-out.

Finished size
Completed toy measures approximately 47cm/18½in from head to foot.

Yarn
Doll: One 50g/1¾oz ball of Rowan *RYC Cashsoft Baby DK* in main color MC (light pink/Imp 803); *or other DK-weight (US light-worsted-weight) yarn in skin color of choice*

Hair and moustache: Small amount of a DK yarn in A (dark brown); *or DK-weight (US light-worsted-weight) yarn in hair color of choice*

Eyebrows: Scrap of a 4-ply yarn in B (grey); *or 4-ply-weight (US fingering weight) yarn in color of choice*

Sweater: One 50g/1¾oz ball of Rowan *RYC Cashsoft Baby DK* in C (very pale green/Chicory 804); *or other DK-weight (US light-worsted-weight) yarn in color of choice*

Bandanna: Small amount of Rowan *Scottish Tweed 4-Ply* in D (tomato/011 Sunset); *or other DK-weight (US fingering-weight) yarn in color of choice*

Belt: Use scraps of some of leftover yarns

Fabric and extras
Felt: Scraps of felt – white for outer eyes, olive green for inner eye, cream and ecru for hat, black and cream for gun; 20cm/8in x 10cm/4in piece of mid brown felt for buttons, chaps, and holster

Embroidery thread: Stranded cotton – black and brown for eyes, nose and mouth

Denim fabric: 40cm/16in x 20cm/8in piece of denim for trousers

Sewing thread: Sewing thread to match felt pieces for gun, holster and trousers

Elastic: Narrow elastic for trouser waistband

Filling: Polyester toy filling

Needles
Pair of 4mm (US size 6) knitting needles
Blunt-ended yarn sewing needle
Embroidery sewing needle
3.00mm (US size D/3) crochet hook

Tension/gauge
Doll and sweater: 22 sts and 30 rows to 10cm/4in measured over st st using 4mm (US size 6) needles and yarn MC or C.

Bandanna: Working to a specific tension/gauge is not essential for bandanna.

Making the **Cowboy**

COWBOY DOLL

To make doll
Using 4mm (US size 6) needles and yarn MC (light pink), make front and back as for Basic Boy Doll on pages 20–22.

Arms and legs
Work arms and legs as for Basic Doll, but make arms 23cm/9in long and legs 28cm/11in long.

To make up
Press front and back of doll lightly on wrong side following instructions on yarn label. Do NOT press arms and legs. Sew on eyes, nose, mouth, moustache, and eyebrows before stitching knitted pieces together.

Eyes
Make up eyes as for Basic Doll, using two strands of black stranded cotton for French knot and for sewing inner eyes in place. Use two strands of brown stranded cotton for sewing outer eyes to doll.

Mouth and nose
Using two strands of brown stranded cotton and embroidery sewing needle, work mouth in chain stitch and nose in split stitch or backstitch as shown.

Moustache
Cut three or four short strands of yarn A (dark brown) for moustache. Using brown stranded cotton and embroidery sewing needle, sew moustache in place at center, positioning it just under nose

Toys like these never leave a child's side; they become part of their being somehow. However old they are, knitted toys always retain that charm.

and above mouth.

Body, head, arms, and legs

Sew together as for Basic Doll.

Eyebrows

Using yarn B (grey) and blunt-ended yarn needle, work eyebrows in stem stitch.

Hair

Using yarn A (dark brown), make a hairpiece with a center or side parting and sew to doll as for Basic Doll. When hair is in place, trim to desired length.

SWEATER

Front

Using 4mm (US size 6) needles and yarn C (very pale green), cast on 26 sts.

Rib row 1 K2, *P2, K2, rep from * to end.

Rib row 2 P2, *K2, P2, rep from * to end.

Last 2 rows forms K2, P2 rib patt.

Work 2 rows more in rib.

Beg with a P row, work 10 rows in rev st st, so ending with a WS (K) row.

Beg square patt as foll:

Patt row 1 (RS) P8, K10, P8.

Patt row 2 K8, P10, K8.

Last 2 rows form square patt.

Work 5 rows more in square patt, so ending with a *RS* row.

Shape raglan armholes

Keeping square patt correct as set, cast off 2 sts at beg of next 2 rows. (22 sts)

Next row (dec row) (WS) K1, K2tog, K3, P10, K3, K2tog, K1. (20 sts)

Next row P5, K10, P5.

Next row (dec row) K1, K2tog, K2, P10, K2, K2tog, K1. (18 sts)

Next row P4, K10, P4.

Next row (dec row) K1, K2tog, K1, P10, K1, K2tog, K1. (16 sts)

Next row P3, K10, P3.

Next row (dec row) K1, K2tog, P10, K2tog, K1. (14 sts)

Next row P2, K10, P2.

Next row (dec row) K2tog, P10, K2tog. (12 sts)

Neck ribbing

Rib row 1 P1, [K2, P2] twice, K2, P1.

Rib row 2 K1, [P2, K2] twice, P2, K1.

Rib row 3 Rep rib row 1.

Cast off in rib.

Back

Using 4mm (US size 6) needles and yarn C (very pale green), cast on 26 sts. Work 4 rows in K2, P2 rib patt as front. Beg with a P row, work in rev st st for 17 rows, so ending with a *RS* (P) row.

Shape raglan armholes

Cont in rev st st, cast off 2 sts at beg of next 2 rows. (22 sts)

Next row (dec row) (WS) K1, K2tog, K to last 3 sts, K2tog, K1. (20 sts)

Purl 1 row.

Rep last 2 rows 3 times more. (14 sts)

Purl 1 row.

Next row (dec row) K1, K2tog, K to last 3 sts, K2tog, K1. (12 sts)

Neck ribbing

Work 3 rows of neck ribbing as for front. Cast off in rib.

Sleeves (make 2)

Using 4mm (US size 6) needles and yarn C (very pale green), cast on 18 sts.

Rib row 1 K2, *P2, K2, rep from * to end.

Rib row 2 P2, *K2, P2, rep from * to end of row.

Last 2 rows form K2, P2 rib patt.

Work 2 rows more in rib.

Change to rev st st and cont as foll:

Next row (inc row) (RS) *P into front and back of st to inc one st—called *Pfb*—, P to last st, Pfb. (20 sts)

Knit 1 row.

Rep last 2 rows once more. (22 sts)

Beg with a P row, work straight in rev st st for 11 rows, so ending with a *RS* (P) row.

Shape raglan sleeve top

Cont in rev st st, cast off 2 sts at beg of next 2 rows. (18 sts)

Next row (dec row) (WS) K1, K2tog, K to last 3 sts, K2tog, K1. (16 sts)

Purl 1 row.

Rep last 2 rows 3 times more. (10 sts)

Next row (dec row) K1, K2tog, K4, K2tog, K1. (8 sts)

Neck ribbing

Rib row 1 P1, K2, P2, K2, P1.

Rib row 2 K1, P2, K2, P2, K1.

Rib row 3 Rep rib row1.

Cast off in rib.

To make up

Press pieces lightly on wrong side following instructions on yarn label. Sew front and back together along side seams. Sew sleeve seams. With sweater wrong side out, sew in sleeves along armhole edges. Turn right side out. Cut out seven 'buttons' from mid brown felt. Using 2 strands of brown stranded cotton and embroidery sewing needle, sew buttons to front of sweater (along edge of stocking/stockinette stitch yoke), with a stitch in center of each.

BANDANNA

To make bandanna

Note: (dc) = US single crochet (sc); (tr) = US double crochet (dc)

Using 3.00mm (US size D-3) crochet hook and yarn D (tomato), make 31ch, leaving a long tail-end of yarn.

Row 1 (WS) 1dc (US single crochet) into 2nd chain from hook, 1dc into each of rem 29ch. Turn. (30dc)

Row 2 1ch, 1dc into each dc to end. Turn.

Row 3 (dec row) 1ch, miss first dc, 1dc into each dc to last 2dc, (insert hook into next dc, yrh and draw a loop through) twice, yrh and draw through all 3 loops on hook. Turn. (28dc)

Row 4 1ch, 1dc into each dc to end. Turn.

Row 5 Rep row 3. (26dc)

Rep last 2 rows 10 times more. (6dc)

Rep row 3 once more. (4dc)

Next row 1ss into each dc to end. Fasten off.

To make up

Press lightly on wrong side following instructions on yarn label.

Sew a length of yarn to end of foundation row, so each end of foundation row has a loose end for tying. When doll is dressed, put bandanna around Cowboy's neck and tie loose ends together at back of neck.

TROUSERS

To make trousers

The stitching details on the trousers were already on the scrap of denim used. However, the effect is easy to achieve by machine stitching lines on the trouser pattern pieces before they are sewn together.

Using matching thread and an embroidery sewing needle or a sewing machine, make the jeans with chaps as follows:

1   Using the pattern-piece templates for the trousers (see page 111), cut out the paper pattern for the trouser tops and chaps.

2   Fold the denim in half widthwise, with right sides together.

3   Pin the pattern piece for the top of the trousers to the double thickness of the denim. Cut out four pieces.

4   With right sides together, pin the two halves of each leg together. Allowing for a 6mm/¼in seam, hand or machine stitch.

5   Turn one trouser leg right side out and place it inside the other leg so that the right sides are together. Align the crotch seams and sew the seam to join the front and back. Turn right side out.

6   Turn under 5mm/¼in twice at the waist to form the waistband casing and stitch in place close to the first fold, leaving an opening to insert the elastic.

7   Thread one end of the elastic through the large-eyed, blunt-ended yarn needle, then insert the needle into the waistband casing at the opening and feed the elastic through waistband (be careful not to lose the end of the elastic inside the waistband). Pull up the elastic to fit around the Cowboy's waist and trim off the ends. Machine or hand stitch the ends of the elastic together very firmly, then tuck the joined ends inside the waistband to conceal them. Stitch the opening closed.

8   Hem, then press the trousers.

9   Pin the pattern pieces for chaps to the mid brown felt and cut out.

10 Fit each chap around the denim legs at the hem and hand stitch in place. Sew on two pairs of thin felt strips to outer of each chap, pinching together the sides of the chaps at the same time.

HAT

To make hat

Using matching thread and an embroidery sewing needle, make the hat as follows:

1   Using the templates for the hat (see page 111), cut the brim pieces from cream felt and the crown pieces from ecru felt.

2   Overcast stitch the crown pieces together along the sides and top, leaving the base edge open. Turn right side out.

3   Sew the short edges of the brim together. Turn right side out.

4   Ease the base edge of the crown to fit inside the hole of the brim, then overcast stitch the brim to the crown inside the hat.

GUN AND HOLSTER

To make gun and holster

Using matching thread and an embroidery sewing needle, make the gun and holster as follows:

1   Using the templates for the gun and holster (see page 111), cut the holster shape from mid brown felt and the gun shapes from black and cream felt.

2   Using running stitch, sew the cream handles to the right side of both gun shapes.

3   With right sides together and using running stitch, sew the black gun shapes together all around the edge.

4   Fold the holster piece in half with wrong sides together and use running stitch to sew the angled sides together.

5   Make a twisted cord from one strand of yarn A (dark brown) and two strands of yarn B (grey) for the belt. Knot the ends, then sew to the holster. Slip the gun into the holster then tie around the cowboy's waist.

Mustang

My children love this very tactile horse. He flops lazily over their arms and they swish his tail. Make him together with the blanket and saddle for that extra role play-ability.

Finished size
Completed toy measures approximately 40cm/15¾in long x 36cm/14¼in tall.

Yarn
Mustang: Four 50g/1¾oz balls of Rowan *Summer Tweed* in main color MC (light grey/Storm 521); *or a DK-weight (US light-worsted-weight) yarn in color of choice*

Muzzle and hooves: One 50g/1¾oz ball of Rowan *Summer Tweed* in A (dark grey/Hurricane 520); *or DK-weight (US light-worsted-weight) yarn in color of choice*

Mane and tail: 25g/1oz ball of Rowan *Kidsilk Haze* in B (mid grey/Smoke 605); *or other lightweight mohair in color of choice*

Stirrups: Scrap of Rowan *Lurex Shimmer* in C (silver/Pewter 333); *or other lightweight silver metallic yarn*

Blanket: One 50g/1¾oz ball of Rowan *RYC Cashsoft DK* in D (mid blue/Mirage 503) for background color, 2 skeins of Anchor wool tapestry yarn in E (terracotta) for border, and a total of 18 skeins of Anchor wool tapestry yarn

for square motifs (choose at least 10 different colors for these); *or other DK-weight (US light-worsted-weight) yarn in colors of choice*

Fabric and extras
Felt: Scraps of felt – cream for outer eyes, brown for inner eyes, black for nostrils; 20cm/8in x 10cm/4in piece of tan felt for saddle

Embroidery thread: Stranded cotton – black for eyes and nostrils, dark grey for eyes, and brown for saddle

Marker pen: Water-soluble fabric marker pen

Sewing thread: Sewing thread to match saddle felt

Filling: Polyester toy filling

Needles and hook
Pair of 3¾mm (US size 5) knitting needles
Blunt-ended yarn sewing needle
Embroidery sewing needle
4.00mm (US size F/5) crochet hook

Tension/gauge
Mustang: 22 sts and 30 rows to 10cm/4in measured over st st

Making the **Mustang**

using 3¾mm (US size 5) needles and yarn MC.

Blanket: Working to a specific tension/gauge is not essential for blanket.

MUSTANG

To make toy

Using 3¾mm (US size 5) needles and yarn A (dark grey) for muzzle and hooves and yarn MC (light grey) for Mustang, make head and body, ears, and legs as for Basic Horse on pages 23–27.

To make up

Press pieces lightly on wrong side following instructions on yarn label.

Head and body

Sew head and body seams as for Basic Horse, using two strands of black stranded cotton for French knot on eyes, two strands of dark grey for sewing inner and outer eyes in place, and two strands of black for sewing on nostrils.

Legs, ears, mane, and tail

Prepare and sew on legs, ears, mane, and tail as for Basic Horse.

SADDLE

To make saddle

Using two strands of brown stranded cotton and an embroidery sewing needle for the decorative seams and matching sewing thread for the other seams, make the saddle as follows:

1   Using the templates for the saddle (see page 111), cut out the paper pattern shapes.

2   Using a water-soluble fabric marker pen, draw around the paper shapes directly onto the tan felt. Cut out the shapes.

3   Pin the back saddle pad and the front saddle pad to the main saddle. Sew the pieces together with running stitches, leaving an opening for inserting the toy filling. Insert toy filling into each pad and sew the opening closed.

4   Couch four strands of stranded cotton around the side flaps and skirt, about 6mm/¼in from the cut edges.

5   Sew the side flaps to the main saddle at the sides, positioning as shown on the templates.

6   For each stirrup, using 3.00mm (US size D/3) crochet hook and yarn C (silver metallic), make 18ch. Fasten off, then stitch the ends of the chain together in a ring.

7   Place the pairs of stirrup straps together and sew together with running stitch, catching in each stirrup at the bottom edges.

8 Sew the stirrup straps to the side flaps.

9 Stitch the whole saddle onto the skirt at the flaps under the main saddle.

BLANKET

Square motifs (make 6)

Note: (dc) = US single crochet (sc); (tr) = US double crochet (dc)

Work each square using a different color skein for each of first 3 rounds. Using 4.00mm (US size F/5) crochet hook and color of choice (color 1), and leaving a long tail-end of yarn (for pulling central hole closed afterwards), make 6ch and join with a ss into first ch to form a ring.

Round 1 (color 1) (RS) Working over tail of yarn end, 3ch, 2tr into ring, 2ch, [3tr into ring, 2ch] 3 times, join with a ss into 3rd of first 3ch. Do not turn at end of rounds, but work with RS always facing.

Break off color 1 and fasten off.

Round 2 (color 2) Join new color yarn with a ss into next 2-ch space (see above left), 3ch, [2tr, 2ch, 3tr] all into same ch space as ss was worked, (see above middle) 1ch, *[3tr, 2ch, 3tr] all in next 2-ch space, 1ch, rep from * twice more, join with a ss into 3rd of first 3ch. Break off color 2 and fasten off.

Round 3 (color 3) Join new color yarn with a ss into next 2-ch space, 3ch, [2tr, 2ch, 3tr] all into same ch space as ss was worked, 1ch, *3tr into next 1-ch space, 1ch, [3tr, 2ch, 3tr] all into next 2-ch space (corner – see above right), 1ch, rep from * twice more, 3tr into next 1-ch space, 1ch, join with a ss into 3rd of first 3ch. Break off color 3 and fasten off.

Round 4 (square edging) Using yarn D (mid blue), join yarn with a ss into any tr of previous round, 1ch, 1dc into same tr as ss was worked, then work 1dc into each tr and each 1-ch space and 3dc into each 2-ch space to end of round, join with a ss into first dc.

Round 5 1ch, 1dc into same place as ss was worked, then work 1dc into each dc along sides and 3dc into each corner dc to end of round, join with a ss into first dc. Fasten off.

To make up

Arrange the squares into two rows of three squares. With right sides together, overcast stitch squares to each other, using matching yarn and blunt-ended yarn needle.

Outer border

Work one round of dc all around outer edge of blanket as foll:

Using yarn E (terracotta), join yarn with a ss into any dc along edge, 1ch, 1dc into same place as ss was worked, then work 1dc into each dc along sides and 3dc into each corner dc to end of round, join with a ss into first dc.

Fasten off.

Weave in any loose ends.

Press pieces lightly on wrong side following instructions on yarn label.

set to sea

Pirate

A jolly, jigging pirate pal with a pet ratty rat is just the toy to accompany your little seafarer on all his journeys in dreams, night or day. It's simple to knit in fine and contrasting chunky yarn. Yo ho!

Finished size

Completed Pirate measures approximately 47cm/18½in from head to foot and Pirate's Ratty approximately 6cm/2½in from nose to tail.

Yarn

Pirate: One 50g/1¾oz ball of Rowan *RYC Cashsoft 4-Ply* in MC (white/Cream 433); *or other 4-ply-weight (US fingering-weight) yarn in skin color of choice*

Hair: One 50g/1¾oz ball of Rowan *Cotton Rope* in A (yellow/Lemonade 060); *or other medium-weight yarn in hair color of choice*

Sock detail on doll: Small amount of Rowan *4-Ply Soft* in B (bright red/Honk 374) used double; *or other 4-ply-weight (US fingering-weight) yarn in color of choice*

Jersey: One 50g/1¾oz ball each of Rowan *Cotton Rope* in C (Black 066) and D (White 067); *or other medium-weight yarn in 2 colors of choice*

Breeches: One 50g/1¾oz ball of Rowan *Denim* in E (dark blue/Memphis 229); *or other DK-weight (US light-worsted-weight) yarn in color of choice*

Braces: Scrap of medium-weight yarn in F (turquoise)

Belt: Small amount of Rowan *4-Ply Soft* in G (dark red/Beetroot 382); *or other 4-ply-weight (US fingering-weight)*

yarn in color of choice

Buckle (and earrings): Small amount of Rowan *Lurex Shimmer* in H (gold/Antique White Gold 332); *or other lightweight gold metallic yarn*

Boots: Small amount of Rowan *4-Ply Cotton* in L (Black 101) and a scrap of 4-ply-weight yarn in M (pale blue); *or other 4-ply-weight (US fingering-weight) yarn in 2 colors of choice*

Hat: One 50g/1¾oz ball of Rowan *Handknit Cotton* in N (bright red/Rosso 215) and leftover white yarn from doll; *or other DK-weight (US light-worsted-weight) yarn in 2 colors of choice*

Eye patch: Use leftover black yarn L (black)

Pirate's Ratty: Small amount of Rowan *4-Ply Soft* in R (dark grey/Sooty 372); *or other 4-ply-weight (US fingering-weight) yarn in color of choice*

Ratty's Scarf: Small amount of leftover yarn N (bright red) and of yarn MC (white)

Fabric and extras

Felt: Scraps of felt – white for Pirate's outer eyes and blue for inner eyes, and circle of grey felt, 2.5cm/1in in diameter

for base of Ratty

Sewing thread: Sewing thread to match grey felt

Embroidery thread:
Stranded cotton – black, grey, and dusty rose pink for whiskers, eyes, noses, and mouths

Filling: Polyester toy filling

Needles and hook

Pair each of 2¾mm, 3¼mm, 4mm, and 4½mm (US sizes 2, 3, 6, and 7) knitting needles

One short double-pointed 4mm (US size 6) knitting needle

4.00mm (US size F/5) crochet hook

Blunt-ended yarn sewing needle

Embroidery sewing needle

Tension/gauge

Pirate Doll and Pirate's Ratty: 30 sts and 38 rows to 10cm/4in measured over st st using 2¾mm (US size 2) needles and yarn MC or R.

Jersey: 16 sts and 27 rows to 10cm/4in measured over garter stitch using 4½mm (US size 7) needles and yarn C or D.

Breeches and hat: 22 sts and 28 rows to 10cm (4in) measured over st st using 4mm (US size 6) needles and yarn E or N.

Boots: 28 sts and 36 rows to 10cm/4in measured over st st using 3¼mm (US size 3) needles and yarn L.

Belt and eye patch: Working to a specific tension/gauge is not essential.

PIRATE DOLL

Front, back, and arms

Using 2¾mm (US size 2) needles and yarn MC (white), make front, back, and arms as for Basic Boy Doll on pages 20–22.

Legs (make 2)

Using 2¾mm (US size 2) needles and yarn B (red), cast on 8 sts.

Beg with a K row, work in st st for 4 rows.

Cont in st st, work 4 rows using yarn MC (white), then 4 rows using yarn B (red).

Rep from ** to ** 3 times more (total of 36 rows worked from cast-on edge).

Break off yarn B and cont with yarn MC only.

Cont in st st until leg measures 26cm/10¼in from cast-on edge, ending with a WS row. Cast off.

(Legs curl into tubes naturally and do not need seaming.)

To make up

Press front and back of doll lightly on wrong side following instructions on yarn label. Do NOT press arms and legs. Sew on eyes, nose, mouth, and whiskers before stitching knitted pieces together.

Eyes

Make up eyes as for Basic Doll, using two strands of black stranded cotton for French knot and for sewing inner eyes in place. Use two strands of dusty rose pink stranded cotton for sewing eyes to doll.

Mouth and nose

Using two strands of dusty rose pink stranded cotton and embroidery sewing needle, work nose in split stitch and mouth in chain stitch as shown.

Whiskers

Using two strands of black stranded cotton and embroidery sewing needle, work whiskers on doll at random in short straight stitches. Change to grey stranded cotton and work more random straight stitches sprinkled around black ones.

Body, head, arms, and legs

Sew together pieces for body and head, and sew on arms and legs as for Basic Doll.

Hair

Using yarn A (yellow), make a hairpiece with a center or side parting and sew to doll as for Basic Doll. When hair is in place, trim to desired length. Then make a single braid at back of head and tie it with a strand of black yarn.

Earrings

Using yarn H (gold metallic) and blunt-ended yarn needle, secure yarn to one side of head, then form a loop and secure in same place. Work second earring in same way on other side of head.

JERSEY

Back and front

Back and front of jersey are worked in one piece.

Using 4½mm (US size 7) needles and yarn C (black), cast on 30 sts.

Rib row 1 (RS) K2, *P2, K2, rep from * to end.

Rib row 2 P2, *K2, P2, rep from * to end.

Last 2 rows form rib patt.

Work 2 rows more in rib patt.

Using yarn D (white), work 2 rows in garter st (knit every row).

Using yarn C, work 2 rows more in garter st.**

Rep from ** to ** once more, so ending with a WS row.

Divide for left back

Next row (RS) Using yarn D, K6 and turn, leaving rem sts on a spare needle. Working on these 6 sts only for left back and cont in garter st stripe patt, work 1 row more in yarn D, 2 rows yarn

Making the **Pirate**

The textures created with the stripy knit and knotty headscarf, chunky gold belt, and denim yarn breeches give this pirate total cuddle-ability.

C, 2 rows yarn D, and 1 row yarn C, so ending with a *RS* row.
Break off yarn D only.

Shape left back shoulder

Next row (WS) Using yarn C, cast off 2 sts, K to end. (4 sts)
Break off yarn C and slip rem 4 sts onto a holder or safety pin for left back neck.

Shape front

With RS facing and using yarn D, rejoin yarn to rem 24 sts, cast off first 4 sts for underarm, K until there are 10 sts on right needle and turn, leaving rem 10 sts on spare needle. (10 sts)
Working on these 10 sts only for front and cont in garter st stripe patt, work 1 row more in yarn D, 2 rows yarn C and 2 rows yarn D, so ending with a WS row.
Break off yarn D only.

Shape front neck

Next row (RS) Using yarn C, K2 and turn, leaving rem 8 front sts on a second spare needle.
Working on these 2 sts only for left front shoulder, work 1 row more in garter st using yarn C.
Cast off k-wise.
With RS facing, slip first 6 sts of rem 8 sts of front onto a holder or safety pin for front neck, then using yarn C rejoin yarn to rem 2 sts of front and K2.
Using yarn C, work 1 row more in garter st. Cast off k-wise.

Right back

With RS facing and using yarn D, rejoin yarn to last 10 sts on first spare needle, cast off first 4 sts for underarm, K to end. (6 sts)
Cont in garter st stripe patt, work 1 row more in yarn D, 2 rows yarn C and 2 rows yarn D, so ending with a WS row.
Break off yarn D only.

Shape right back shoulder

Next row (RS) Using yarn C, cast off 2

sts, K to end.
Break off yarn C and slip rem 4 sts onto a holder or safety pin for right back neck.

Sleeves (make 2)

Using 4½mm (US size 7) needles and yarn C (black), cast on 14 sts.
Work 2 rows in rib as given for back and front.
**Using yarn D (white), work 2 rows in garter st.
Using yarn C, work 2 rows more in garter st.**
Rep from ** to ** 6 times more.
Cast off k-wise.

To make up

Do NOT press.
With RS together and using white yarn, sew 2-st shoulder seams.

Neckband

With RS facing and using yarn D (white), K 4 sts of left back neck from holder, pick up and K 5 sts across shoulder seam and down left side of front neck, K 6 sts of front neck from holder, pick up and K 5 sts up right side of front neck and across shoulder seam, then K 4 sts of right back neck from holder. (24 sts)
Rib row 1 (WS) K2, P2, rep from * to end.
Rep last row 3 times more.
Cast off in rib.
Sew center back and neckband seam.
Sew sleeve seams, then ease sleeves into armholes and sew in place with backstitch.

BREECHES

Front and back (both alike)

Front is begun at bottom of legs; each leg is worked separately and they are joined at crotch.

First leg

Using 4mm (US size 6) needles and yarn E (dark blue), cast on 14 sts.
Beg with a K row, work in st st until leg measures 15cm/6in from cast-on edge (about 44 rows), ending with a WS row.
Break off yarn and slip sts onto a double-pointed needle.

Second leg

Make second leg in exactly same way as first, but do NOT break off yarn.

Join legs

Knit across 14 sts of second leg, then with RS facing, knit across 14 sts of first leg. (28 sts)
Beg with a P row, work 13 rows in st st, so ending with WS row.

Shape waist

Next row (dec row) K8, K2tog, K to last 10 sts, K2tog, K8. (26 sts)
Purl 1 row.
Next row K7, K2tog, K to last 9 sts, K2tog, K7. (24 sts)
Purl 1 row.
Next row K6, K2tog, K to last 8 sts, K2tog, K6. (22 sts)
Beg with a P row, work straight in st st for 5 rows, so ending with a WS row.
Cast off.

Braces (make 2)

Using 4.00mm (US size F/5) crochet hook and yarn F (turquoise), make 20ch.
Fasten off.

To make up

Press front and back of breeches lightly on wrong side following instructions on yarn label.
With RS together, sew front of breeches to back along inside leg and sides.
Weave in all loose ends. Turn right side out.
Sew ends of braces to side seams

inside breeches waistband, crossing them over at back.

BELT

To make belt
Using 3¼mm (US size 3) needles and 2 strands of yarn G (red) held tog, cast on 46 sts.
Work in moss stitch as foll:
Patt row 1 *K1, P1, rep from * to end.
Patt row 2 *P1, K1, rep from * to end.
Patt row 3 Rep patt row 1.
Cast off in moss st.

Buckle
Using 3¼mm (US 3) needles and yarn H (gold metallic), cast on 7 sts.
Work buckle in garter st (knit every row) as foll:
Row 1 K to end.
Row 2 K2, cast off 3 sts, K to end. (4 sts)
Row 3 K2, cast on 3 sts over those cast off in last row, K2.
Row 4 K to end.
Rep rows 2–3 once more.
Cast off k-wise.

To make up
Do NOT press. Sew buckle to one end of belt.

BOOTS

Soles (make 2)
Using 3¼mm (US size 3) needles and yarn L (black), cast on 3 sts.
Row 1 (WS) P to end.
Row 2 (inc row) K1, *K into front and back of next st to inc one st—called *Kfb*—, rep from * once more. (5 sts)
Row 3 (inc row) *P1, P into front and back of next st to inc one st—called

Pfb—, rep from * once more, P1. (7 sts)
Beg with a K row, work straight in st st for 4 rows, so ending with a WS row.
Next row (dec row) K2tog, K3, K2tog. (5 sts)
Purl 1 row.
Next row (dec row) K2tog, K1, K2tog. (3 sts)
Purl 1 row.
Break off yarn leaving a long tail-end, then thread yarn end onto a blunt-ended yarn needle and pass yarn needle through rem 3 sts as they are slipped off knitting needle. Pull tight to gather sts and secure.

Uppers (make 2)
Using 3¼mm (US size 3) needles and yarn L (black), cast on 24 sts.
Work 2 rows in garter st (knit every row).
Next row (dec row) K2tog, K to last 2 sts, K2tog. (22 sts)
Rep last row 5 times more. (12 sts)
Work straight in garter st for 2 rows.
Next row (inc row) K1, Kfb, K to last 2 sts, Kfb, K1. (14 sts)
Rep last row 6 times more. (26 sts)
Cast off k-wise.

To make up
With RS together, sew cast-off edge of uppers to soles. Then sew front seams on uppers, leaving top ten rows free. Use a strand of yarn M (pale blue) to lace up boots, then tie ends in a bow.

HAT

To make hat
Using 4mm (US size 6) needles and yarn N (red), cast on 40 sts.
Beg with a K row, work in st st until hat measures 7.5cm/3in from cast-on edge, ending with a WS row.

Next row (dec row) (RS) *K2tog, rep from * to end. (20 sts)
Next row (dec row) *P2tog, rep from * to end. (10 sts)
Beg with a K row, work straight in st st until hat measures 18cm/7in from cast-on edge.
Break off yarn leaving a long tail-end, then thread yarn end onto a blunt-ended yarn needle and pass yarn needle through rem 10 sts as they are slipped off knitting needle. Pull tight to gather sts and secure.

To make up
Press lightly on wrong side following instructions on yarn label, but avoid rolled edge at cast-on end.
Sew back hat seam. Put hat on doll, allow top to flop over to side and pin top to side of hat. Take hat off doll and secure top of hat in position at side of hat with a couple stitches.
Using yarn MC (white), work French knots or tiny straight stitches at random on hat to form polka dots.

EYE PATCH

Patch
Using 4mm (US size 6) needles and 2 strands yarn L (black) held tog, cast on 2 sts.
Row 1 (inc row) *K into front and back of st to inc one st—called *Kfb*—, rep from * once more. (4 sts)
Row 2 (inc row) Kfb into every st. (8 sts)
Rep last row once more. (16 sts)
Work straight in garter st (knit every row) for 3 rows.
Next row (dec row) *K2tog, rep from * to end. (8 sts)
Rep last row once more. (4 sts)

Chunky, laced-up hobnailed boots and a lopsided eye-patch, gold earrings, and stripy hose make for a jaunty characterful pirate. Fearsome or friendly? The choice is yours.

Break off yarn leaving a long tail-end, then thread yarn end onto a blunt-ended yarn needle and pass yarn needle through rem 4 sts as they are slipped off knitting needle. Pull tight to gather sts and secure.

Eye-patch cord

Using 4.00mm (US size F/5) crochet hook and yarn L (black), make 20ch. Fasten off.

To make up

Do NOT press.

Overcast stitch patch to chain about one third from one end.

Position hat on doll's head, then place eye patch tightly around bottom of hat (just above curled edge) to test length of cord. Sew ends of cord together.

PIRATE'S RATTY

Body

Using 2¾mm (US size 2) needles and yarn R (dark grey), cast on 20 sts.

Row 1 (WS) P to end.

Row 2 (dec row) K2tog, K to last 2 sts, K2tog. (18 sts)

Rep rows 1 and 2 five times more, so ending with a *RS* row. (8 sts)

Beg with a P row, work straight in st st for 5 rows, so ending with a WS row.

Next row (dec row) (RS) K2tog, K4, K2tog. (6 sts)

Purl 1 row.

Next row (dec row) K2tog, K2, K2tog. (4 sts)

Purl 1 row.

Next row (dec row) [K2tog] twice. (2 sts)

Break off yarn leaving a long tail-end, then thread yarn end onto a blunt-ended yarn needle and pass yarn needle through rem 2 sts as they are slipped off knitting needle. Pull tight to gather and secure.

Ears (make 2)

Using 2¾mm (US size 2) needles and yarn R (dark grey), cast on 2 sts.

Row 1 (inc row) (RS) K into front and back of st to inc one st—called *Kfb*—, K1. (3 sts)

Row 2 P to end.

Row 3 [Kfb] twice, K1. (5 sts)

Beg with a P row, work straight in st st for 5 rows.

Break off yarn leaving a long tail-end, then thread yarn end onto a blunt-ended yarn needle and pass yarn needle through rem 5 sts as they are slipped off knitting needle. Pull tight to gather sts and secure.

To make up

Press lightly on wrong side following instructions on yarn label.

Using blunt-ended yarn needle and matching yarn and with RS together, sew row-end edges of body together along center front seam, leaving cast-on edge at base open. Turn right side out. Turn mouse upside down and insert filling through base. Then ease cast-on edge to fit felt circle base and overcast stitch felt in place, using matching sewing thread and embroidery sewing needle.

Nose, eyes, and whiskers

Using embroidery sewing needle and two strands of black stranded cotton, embroider nose in satin stitch at tip of toy, work French knots for eyes and secure long strands for whiskers as shown.

Tail

For tail, cut a 30cm/12in length of yarn A (dark grey). Twist strand tightly, then fold in half to make a twisted cord. Knot cut end of cord, then sew folded end to cast-on edge of mouse.

Ears

Overcast stitch ears to either side of the head as shown.

RATTY'S SCARF

To make scarf

Using 2¾mm (US size 2) needles and yarn N (red), cast on 1 st.

Row 1 (inc row) K into front and back of st to inc one st—called *Kfb*. (2 sts)

Row 2 P2.

Row 3 [Kfb] twice. (4 sts)

Row 4 P to end.

Row 5 Kfb, K to last st, Kfb. (6 sts)

Rep rows 4 and 5 seven times more, so ending with a *RS* row. (20 sts)

Work straight in garter st (knit every row) for 2 rows.

Cast off k-wise.

To make up

Using blunt-ended yarn needle and 2 strands of yarn MC (white), sew on tiny straight stitches at random over scarf to form polka dots.

Wrap scarf around Ratty's neck and secure at front with a couple stitches.

Although tiny, this little ratty chap is so characterful that you may like to knit him as a toy on his own. Simple and quick to make, he would make a perfect first knitting experience for your child.

Dinghy

Fuel their magical imagination with this simple crocheted dinghy. The oars and the mast are stiffened with drinking straws.

Finished size

Completed toy measures approximately 23cm/9in long x 10cm/4in wide, measured across longest and widest parts but excluding mast and oars.

Yarn

Boat: One ball 50g/1¾ ball of Rowan *Cotton Glace* in A (red/Poppy 741) and one ball in B (green/Shoot 814); *or other medium-weight cotton yarn in two colors of choice*

Oars: Small amount each of Rowan *RYC Cashcotton DK* in C (pale blue/Cool 601) and Rowan *RYC Cashsoft DK* in D (white/Cream 500); *or other DK-weight (US light-worsted-weight) yarn in 2 colors of choice*

Mast: Small amount of Rowan *Handknit Cotton* in E (dark brown/ Double Chocolate 315); *or other DK-weight (US light-worsted-weight) yarn in color of choice*

Sail: Small amount of Rowan *RYC Cashsoft DK* in F (Black 519) and leftover of yarn D; *or other DK-weight (US light-worsted-weight) yarn in 2 colors of choice*

Extras

Four drinking straws for stiffening mast and oars

Needles and hook

Pair of 3¼mm (US size 3) knitting needles
Blunt-ended yarn sewing needle
4.00mm (US size F/5) crochet hook

Tension/gauge

Working to a specific tension/gauge is not essential for this toy.

Boat

Note: (dc) = US single crochet (sc)
Boat is made in one piece as foll:
Using 4.00mm (US size F/5) crochet hook and yarn A (red), make 19ch.
Row 1 (RS) 1dc into 2nd ch from hook, 1dc into each of rem 17ch. Turn. (18dc)
(Mark last row as *RS* of piece.)
Shape bow and stern
Inc one st at each end of each row as foll:
**Row 2 1ch, 2dc into first dc, 1dc into each dc to last dc, 2dc into last dc. Turn. (20dc)
Rep last row 3 times more. (26dc)

Break off yarn A.

Next row Using yarn B (green), rep row 2. (28dc)

Rep last row 3 times more. (34dc) Fasten off.**

Turn piece around so that you can work into other side of foundation ch that row 1 was worked into.

With *RS* facing and using yarn A, rejoin yarn to first ch of foundation-ch and work 1ch, 1dc into same place as 1ch was worked into, then 1dc into each of rem 17ch along this edge. (18dc)

Rep from ** to ** to complete second side of boat.

Oar shanks (make 2)

Using 3¼mm (US size 3) needles and yarn C (pale blue), cast on 5 sts.

Beg with a K row, work in st st until shank measures 14cm/5½in from cast-on edge, ending with a WS row.

Cast off.

Oar blades (make 2)

Using 3¼mm (US size 3) needles and yarn D (off-white), cast on 1 st.

Row 1 K into front, back and front of st. (3 sts)

Row 2 P3.

Row 3 K into front and back of st to inc one st—called *Kfb*—, K to last st, Kfb. (5 sts)

Beg with a P row, work straight in st st for 17 rows, so ending with a WS row.

Next row K2tog, K1, K2 tog. (3 sts)

Purl 1 row.

Break off yarn leaving a long tail-end, then thread yarn end onto a blunt-ended yarn needle and pass yarn needle through rem 3 sts as they are slipped off knitting needle.

Pull tight to gather and leave tail-end to sew seam later.

Mast

Using 3¼mm (US size 3) needles and yarn E (dark brown), cast on 5 sts.

Beg with a K row, work in st st until mast measures 20cm/8in from cast-on edge, ending with a WS row. Cast off.

Mast crossbar

Work crossbar as for mast, but make it 9cm/3½in long.

Sail

Using 3¼mm (US size 3) needles and yarn D (white), cast on 19 sts.

Beg with a K row, work 20 rows in st st, so ending with a WS row.

Cast off.

Buoy

Note: (dc) = US single crochet (sc) Using 4.00mm (US size F/5) crochet hook and yarn D (white), make 2ch.

Round 1 (RS) Work 6dc into 2nd ch from hook, join with a ss into top of first dc. Do not turn at end of rounds, but work with RS always facing.

Round 2 1ch, 2dc into same place as ss, 2dc into each of rem 5dc of round, join with a ss into first dc of round. (12dc)

Round 3 1ch, 1dc into same place as ss, 1dc into each of rem 11dc of round, join with a ss into first dc of round. (12dc)

Round 4 1ch, 1dc into same place as ss, *2dc into next dc, 1dc into next dc, rep from * to last dc, 2dc into last dc, join with a ss into first dc of round. (18dc)

Round 5 Rep round 3. (18dc)

Round 6 1ch, 1dc into same place as ss, *miss next dc, 1dc into next dc, rep from * to last dc, join with a ss into first dc of round. (9dc)

Round 7 1ch, 1dc into same place as ss, *miss next dc, 1dc into next dc, rep from * to end of round, join with a ss into first dc of round. (5dc)

Fasten off, leaving a very long tail-end of yarn. Using yarn tail and a blunt-ended yarn needle, sew together opening on buoy, then use same yarn to work 10ch. Fasten off.

To make up

Press pieces lightly on wrong side following instructions on yarn label. Use a blunt-ended yarn needle and matching yarn to sew all seams.

Boat

With WS together and using 4.00mm (US size F/5) crochet hook and yarn B (green), join together boat ends by working dc (US single crochet) through both layers along tapered row-end edges at bow and stern. Fasten off and weave in ends.

Oar slots

Thread a blunt-ended yarn needle with a 30cm/12in length of yarn B (green) and secure yarn to wrong side of 15th stitch on top of one side of boat. Then secure yarn to 18th dc, leaving a loop big enough to push three fingers through at once. Double loop by passing yarn back to 15th stitch and securing there again. Work buttonhole stitch closely together along loop to cover it and secure yarn on wrong side of boat. Make second oar slot in same way on other side of boat.

Oars

With wrong sides together, sew together row-end edges of one oar shank. Cut a drinking straw to same length as oar shank, push it into shank and sew together cast-on and cast-off ends to enclose straw inside shank.

With wrong sides together, fold one oar blade in half widthwise and overcast stitch sides together. Sew narrow end of blade to cast-off end of prepared shank. Bind join between oar blade and shank with a length of yarn E (dark brown) and secure ends.

Complete other oar in same way and insert oars into oar slots.

Mast

Prepare mast and crossbar as for the oar shank.

Attach crossbar to mast by criss-crossing a length of matching yarn around them until they feel firmly fastened, then secure yarn end.

Sew mast to inside of boat at stern end, pinching end of boat together to straighten it.

Sail

Using a blunt-ended yarn needle and yarn F (black), Swiss darn/duplicate stitch chart pattern onto sail (see page 112). Tie top two corners of sail to mast with short lengths of yarn D (off-white).

Buoy

Attach end of buoy chain to inside of stern of Dinghy as shown.

magical
waterworld

Mermaid

There is nothing more enchanting than the idea of beautiful mermaids living under the surface of the sea in a magical underwater world. This is how I imagine they look.

Finished size

Completed toy measures approximately 42cm/16½in from head to tip of tail.

Yarn

Doll: One 50g/1¾oz ball of Jaeger *Baby Merino 4-Ply* in MC (light pink/ Dream 123); *or other 4-ply-weight (US fingering-weight) yarn in skin color of choice*

Hair: One 50g/1¾oz ball of Rowan *All Seasons Cotton* in A (mottled tangerine/Printed Keen 210); *or other medium-weight yarn in color of choice*

Tail: One 50g/1¾oz ball of Rowan *Summer Tweed* in B (light green/Dew 513); *or a DK-weight (US light-worsted-weight) yarn in color of choice*

Tail fins: Small amount of Rowan *RYC Cashcotton DK* in C (pale blue/Cool 601); *or other DK-weight (US light-worsted-weight) yarn in color of choice*

Waist ruffle and tail scallops: Small amount of Rowan *4-Ply Cotton* in D (coral/Tutti Fruiti 138); *or other 4-ply (US fingering-weight) yarn in color of choice*

Tankini: Small amount of Jaeger *Baby Merino 4-Ply* in E (tangerine/Marigold 096); *or other 4-ply (US fingering-weight) yarn in color of choice*

Fabric and extras

Felt: Scraps of felt – white for outer eyes, green for inner eyes, and light pink for mouth

Embroidery thread: Stranded cotton – black for eyes, light pink for mouth and nose; light blue, pale pink, and red for shell decorations and pale coral for starfish decorations (or use 4-ply yarn for these decorations)

Filling: Polyester toy filling

Needles

Pair each of 2¾mm and 5mm (US sizes 2 and 8) knitting needles
Blunt-ended yarn sewing needle
Embroidery sewing needle

Tension/gauge

Doll, tail fins and tankini:
30 sts and 38 rows to 10cm/4in measured over st st using 2¾mm (US size 2) needles and yarn MC, C or E.

Tail: 16 sts and 23 rows to 10cm/4in measured over st st using 5mm (US size 8) needles and yarn B.

MERMAID DOLL

Front, back, and arms

Using 2¾mm (US size 2) needles and yarn MC (light pink), make front, back, and arms as for Basic Girl Doll on pages 20–22, omitting legs.

Tail

Tail is worked in one piece (with a waist ruffle and scalloped edgings sewn around tail afterwards).

Using 5mm (US size 8) needles and yarn B (light green), cast on 3 sts.

Beg with a K row, work 2 rows in st st, so ending with a WS row.

Next row (inc row) (RS) *K into front and back of next st to inc one st—called *Kfb*—, rep from * to end. (6 sts)

Purl 1 row.

Next row (inc row) *Kfb, rep from * to end. (12 sts)

Next row (inc row) P into front and back of next st to inc one st—called *Pfb*—, P to last st, Pfb. (14 sts)

Next row (inc row) Kfb, K to last st, Kfb. (16 sts)

Beg with a P row, work straight in st st for 15 rows, so ending with a WS row.

Next row (inc row) (RS) *Kfb, rep from * to end. (32 sts)

Beg with a P row, work straight in st st for 35 rows, so ending with a WS row.

Next row (dec row) (RS) *K1, K2tog, rep from * to last 2 sts, K2. (22 sts)

Cast off p-wise.

Tail fins (make 4)

Using 2¾mm (US size 2) needles and yarn C (pale blue), cast on 5 sts.

Rib row 1 [K1, P1] twice, K1.

Rib row 2 [P1, K1] twice, P1.

Last 2 rows set K1, P1 rib patt.

Cont in rib as set, inc one st at each

end of next row and every foll alt row until there are 21 sts, taking extra sts into patt.

Work straight in K1, P1 rib for 12 rows.

Cont in rib as set, dec one st at each end of next row and every foll alt row until 5 sts rem.

Next row (dec row) K2tog, K1, K2tog. (3 sts)

Cast off k-wise.

Waist ruffle

Using 2¾mm (US size 2) needles and yarn D (coral), cast on 141 sts.

Row 1 K1, *K2, slip first stitch on right needle over second st and off needle, rep from * to end. (71 sts)

Row 2 P1, *P2tog, rep from * to end. (36 sts)

Beg with a K row, work straight in st st for 2 rows, so ending with a WS row. Cast off.

First scalloped edging

Using 2¾mm (US size 2) needles and yarn D (coral), cast on 46 sts.

Row 1 P to end.

Row 2 K2, *K1 and slip st just knit back onto left needle, lift next 8 sts one at a time over this st and off left needle, yfwd (to make a yarn-over on right needle), K first st again, K2, rep from * to end. (18 sts)

Row 3 *K1, P1, rep from * to end.

Cast off.

Second scalloped edging

Using 2¾mm (US size 2) needles and yarn D (coral), cast on 68 sts.

Work rows 1–3 of first scalloped edging. (26 sts) Cast off.

Third scalloped edging

Using 2¾mm (US size 2) needles and

yarn D (coral), cast on 101 sts.
Work rows 1–3 of first scalloped
edging. (38 sts)
Cast off.

Fourth scalloped edging

Using 2¾mm (US size 2) needles and
yarn D (coral), cast on 112 sts.
Work rows 1–3 of first scalloped
edging. (42 sts)
Cast off.

Shell decorations

Using six strands of red stranded cotton
(or a single strand of 4-ply yarn) and an
embroidery sewing needle, work bullion
knots to form a shell decoration on the
tail piece near the waist end (refer to
photo for position) as follows:

1 Secure the thread at the back of the
   knitting and bring the needle through
   to the front in the center of the shell
   (see A on next page).
2 Insert the needle through to the
   back about 1cm/⅜in from where it
   first emerged (B) and bring it
   through to the front again at the
   same place where it first emerged
   (A).
3 Evenly wind the thread ten times
   around the needle, ensuring that the
   wraps sit close together.
4 Ease the wrapped coil down the
   needle towards the surface of the
   fabric with your forefinger and
   thumb. Then holding the coil firmly,
   pull the working thread taut and
   gently pull the needle and working
   thread through the coil.
5 Pull the thread away from you to
   ensure a tight, even knot. To secure
   the coil, insert the needle through
   to the back of the knitting at the end
   of the knot (B) and secure.

Captured for a brief moment from a tropical
ocean blue, a beautiful mermaid has many
tales to tell of that magical world from whence
she came.

6 Tease the coil to make it even.

7 Work another knot in the same way next to the first.

8 To create the shell curve, work two more knots at either side of the first two and at slight angles.

9 To complete the shell, work three satin stitches at the base of the knots (A) to form the base of the shell.

Starfish decoration

Using an embroidery sewing needle and six strands of pale coral stranded cotton (or a single strand of 4-ply yarn), work a starfish on front of tail in position shown. Work starfish as for shell, but instead of bunching knots together, work five knots radiating out around center point (A).

To make up

Press front and back of doll, tail, and tail fins lightly on wrong side following instructions on yarn label. Do NOT press arms.

Sew on eyes, nose, and mouth before stitching knitted pieces together.

Eyes

Make up eyes as for Basic Doll, using two strands of black stranded cotton for French knots and for sewing inner and outer eyes in place.

Mouth and nose

Cut out piece of light pink felt for mouth, using template (see page 110). Using two strands of light pink stranded cotton and an embroidery sewing needle, sew on mouth with tiny running stitches and work two straight stitches on top of each other for nose.

Body, head, arms, and legs

Sew together pieces for body and head, and sew on arms as for Basic Doll.

Hair

Using yarn A (mottled tangerine), make a hairpiece with a center parting and sew to doll as for Basic Doll.

Work a decorative shell in hair as for shell on tail, but using six strands of light blue stranded cotton (or a single strand of 4-ply yarn). Work a second shell along hair strands using red.

Scalloped edgings

Arrange scalloped edgings along tail piece so that they are evenly spaced, positioning shortest (first scalloped edging) near tip of tail and positioning three longer edgings to match tail shape. Pin in place with row-end edges of edgings aligned with row-end edges of tail. Using a blunt-ended yarn needle and matching yarn, sew edgings in place.

Tail
With RS facing, sew back seam of tail, catching ends of scalloped edgings into seam. Turn right side out.

Waist ruffle
Sew waist ruffle to top edge of tail.

Tail fins
Using a blunt-ended yarn needle and matching yarn, sew tail-fin pieces together in pairs to make two fins, leaving a small opening for inserting filling. Fill lightly with toy filling and sew opening closed. Sew tail fins to tip of tail. Fill tail with toy filling, then sew it to Mermaid's body.

Belly button
Using a blunt-ended yarn needle and yarn MC (light pink), work a French knot on doll for belly button.

TANKINI

Back and front (both alike)
Using 5mm (US size 8) needles and yarn E (tangerine), cast on 60 sts.
Beg with a P row, work 3 rows in st st, so ending with a WS row.
Next row (dec row) (RS) *K2tog, rep from * to end. (30 sts)
Purl 1 row.
Next row (dec row) K1, *K5, K2tog, rep from * to last st, K1. (26 sts)
Beg with a P row, work straight in st st for 3 rows.
Next row (dec row) K5, *K2tog, K5, rep from * to end. (23 sts)
Beg with a P row, work straight in st st for 5 rows, so ending with a WS row.

Shape armholes and straps
Cont in st st, cast off 2 sts at beg of each of next 2 rows, so ending with a WS row. (19 sts)
Next row (RS) K4, cast off next 11 sts for neck, K to end and turn.
Working only on first 4 sts on left needle for first strap and beg with a P row, work straight in st st for 5 rows, so ending with a WS row. Cast off.
With WS facing and using yarn E, rejoin yarn to rem 4 sts and P to end.
Beg with a K row, work straight in st st for 4 rows, so ending with a WS row. Cast off.

To make up
Press lightly on wrong side following instructions on yarn label.
Sew side and shoulder strap seams with mattress stitch.
Work a shell decoration on front of tankini as for shell on tail, but using pale pink stranded cotton (or 4-ply yarn).
Work a second shell near back neck edge, but using pale blue.

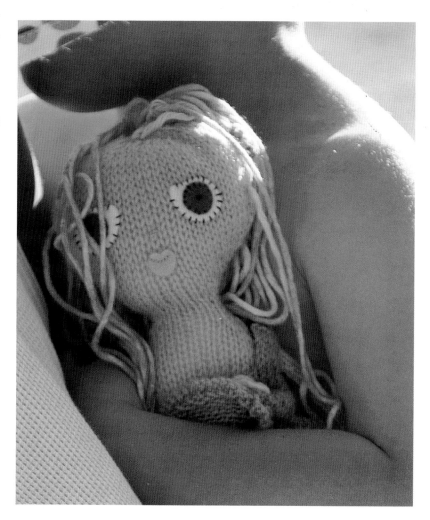

Fish, seahorses, and crab

Children love mermaids' friends. They are very quick and easy to knit, so make lots of them in a whole variety of colors. I used tapestry yarn for these because of the huge color range available.

Finished sizes

Fish: Completed toy measures approximately 11.5cm/4½in from tip of nose to tip of tail.

Sea horse: Completed toy measures approximately 15cm/6in from tip of nose to tip of tail.

Crab: Body of completed Crab measures approximately 4.5cm/1¾in in diameter.

Yarn

Use skeins of Anchor wool tapestry yarn in quantities specified below for each fish, and small amounts of DK-weight yarn for seahorses and crab; *or use other DK-weight (US light-worsted-weight) yarn in colors of choice*

Orange spotted fish: Two skeins of orange and one skein each of light brown, lilac, turquoise, white, and black

Turquoise and yellow fish: Two skeins of turquoise and one skein each of black, pale yellow, and white

Yellow, black, and white fish: Two skeins of yellow and one skein each of white and black

Black and white fish: Two skeins of black and one skein each of white, hot pink, pale yellow, and orange

Blue sea horse: Turquoise, mid blue, green, hot pink, white, and black

Pink sea horse: Hot pink, rust, light coral, white, and black

Crab: Yellow, pale ochre, white, orange, and black

Extras

Crab legs: Scrap of light coral 4-ply cotton yarn for crab legs

Filling: Polyester toy filling

Needles

Pair of 3¼mm (US size 3) knitting needles
Blunt-ended yarn sewing needle

Tension/gauge

Working to a specific tension/gauge is not essential for these toys.

ORANGE SPOTTED FISH

To make fish

Beg at tail end of fish as foll:
Using 3¼mm (US size 3) needles and light brown yarn, cast on 4 sts.
Break off light brown.

Shape tail

Using lilac yarn, work tail in st st as foll:

Row 1 (RS) K to end.

Row 2 (inc row) P to last st, P into front and back of st to inc one st—called *Pfb*. (5 sts)

Rep last 2 rows once more, so ending with a WS (P) row. (6 sts)

Knit 1 row. Break off lilac yarn.

Shape body

Using orange yarn, cont as foll:

Next row (WS) Cast on and P 6 sts, P to end. (12 sts)

Next row (inc row) (RS) *K into front and back of st to inc one st—called *Kfb*, K to last st, Kfb. (14 sts)

Purl 1 row.

Rep last 2 rows 3 times more, so ending with a WS row. (20 sts)

Next row (inc row) (RS) Kfb, K to last st, Kfb. (22 sts)

Making the **Fish, seahorses, and crab**

Beg with a P row, work straight in st st for 13 rows, so ending with a WS row.

Shape nose

Next row (dec row) (RS) Cast off first 8 sts k-wise, K to last 8 sts, cast off last 8 sts and fasten off. (6 sts)

With WS facing, rejoin orange yarn and P to end.

Next row (dec row) (WS) K2tog, K2, K2tog. (4 sts)

Break off yarn, leaving a long tail-end, then thread yarn end onto a blunt-ended yarn needle and pass yarn needle through rem 4 sts as they are slipped off knitting needle. Leave tail-end loose for sewing mouth.

To make up

Press fish lightly on wrong side, following instructions on yarn label. Using blunt-ended yarn needle and matching yarn for all seams, sew seams as follows:

Fold fish in half lengthwise, with right sides together and aligning row-end edges. Sew forehead seam with backstitch, then turn right side out. Refold fish in half lengthwise, but with wrong sides together. Backstitch seam along backbone and tail, working 6mm/¼in from edge along top of fish (to form a fin top). Insert filling and complete seam by sewing cast-on edge above tail to WS of tail. Form end of nose into an O-shape and sew in place.

Top fringe

Cut 11 strands of lilac yarn, each 13cm/5in long. Fold one strand in half, thread fold through a blunt-ended yarn needle and slide needle along to opposite end of yarn. Beginning at front of fish on top of head, insert needle in and out through backbone edge and as needle emerges, pass it through loop at

folded end of strand. Pull loop down to top of head to secure, then slip off needle. Sew on remaining 10 strands of fringe like this all along backbone, placing fringe close together. Trim completed fringe as shown.

Eyes and side fins

Using blunt-ended yarn needle and white yarn, work a satin stitch eye at each side of head, then complete with a black French knot in center.

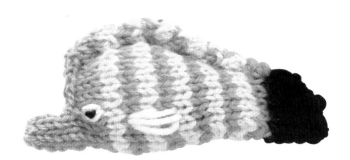

Using white yarn, work four long stitches for side fins. Using turquoise yarn, embroider French knot spots all over body.

TURQUOISE AND YELLOW FISH

To make fish

Beg at tail end of fish as foll:

Using 3¼mm (US size 3) needles and black yarn, cast on 4 sts.

Shape tail

Work tail in st st as foll:

Row 1 (WS) P to end.

Row 2 (inc row) K to last st, K into front and back of st to inc one st—called *Kfb*. (5 sts)

Rep last 2 rows once more, so ending with a *RS* row. (6 sts)

Purl 1 row.

Break off black yarn.

Shape body

Change to st st and stripes; cont as foll:

Next row (inc row) (RS) Using turquoise yarn, cast on and K 6 sts, K to end. (12 sts)

Using turquoise yarn, purl 1 row.

Next row (inc row) Using pale yellow yarn, Kfb, K to last st, Kfb. (14 sts)

Using pale yellow yarn, purl 1 row.

Rep last 4 rows twice more, so ending

with a WS row. (22 sts)

Using turquoise yarn and beg with a K row, work straight in st st for 2 rows. Using pale yellow yarn and beg with a K row, work straight in st st for 2 rows. Rep from ** to ** once more, so ending with a WS row.

Break off pale yellow yarn.

Cont with turquoise yarn only and beg with a K row, work straight in st st for 4 rows, so ending with a WS row.

Shape nose

Next row (dec row) (RS) Cast off first 8 sts k-wise, K to last 8 sts, cast off last 8 sts and fasten off. (6 sts)

With WS facing, rejoin turquoise yarn and P to end.

Beg with a K row, work straight in st st for 4 rows, so ending with a WS row.

Next row (dec row) (WS) K2tog, K2, K2tog. (4 sts)

Break off yarn, leaving a long tail-end, then thread yarn end onto a blunt-ended yarn needle and pass yarn needle through rem 4 sts as they are slipped off knitting needle. Pull tight to gather and secure with a few sts.

To make up

Make up as for Orange Spotted Fish, but omit fringe and spots.

YELLOW, BLACK AND WHITE FISH

To make fish

Beg at tail end of fish as foll:
Using 3¼mm (US size 3) needles and white yarn, cast on 4 sts.

Shape tail

Work tail in st st as foll:

Row 1 (WS) P to end.

Row 2 (inc row) K to last st, K into front and back of st to inc one st—called *Kfb*. (5 sts)

Rep last 2 rows once more, so ending with a *RS* row. (6 sts)

Purl 1 row.

Shape body

Change to stripes and cont as foll:

Next row (inc row) (RS) Using black yarn, cast on and K 6 sts, K to end. (12 sts)

Using yellow yarn, purl 1 row.

Next row (inc row) Using yellow yarn,

Kfb, K to last st, Kfb. (14 sts)
Using yellow yarn, purl 1 row.

Next row (inc row) Using white yarn, Kfb, K to last st, Kfb. (16 sts)
Using white yarn, purl 1 row.

Next row (inc row) Using white yarn, Kfb, K to last st, Kfb. (18 sts)
Using black yarn, purl 1 row.

Next row (inc row) Using yellow yarn, Kfb, K to last st, Kfb. (20 sts)
Using yellow yarn, purl 1 row.

Next row (inc row) Using white yarn, Kfb, K to last st, Kfb. (22 sts)
Beg with a P row, work straight in st st, working in stripes as foll:
1 row white, 2 rows yellow, 2 rows white, 1 row black, 5 rows yellow, so ending with a WS row.

Shape nose

Cont with yellow yarn only as foll:

Next row (dec row) (RS) Cast off first 8 sts k-wise, K to last 8 sts, cast off last 8 sts and fasten off. (6 sts)
With WS facing, rejoin yellow yarn and P to end.
Beg with a K row, work straight in st st for 2 rows, so ending with a WS row.

Next row (dec row) (WS) K2tog, K2, K2tog. (4 sts)
Break off yarn, leaving a long tail-end, then thread yarn end onto a blunt-ended yarn needle and pass yarn needle through rem 4 sts as they are slipped off knitting needle. Pull

tight to gather sts and secure with a few sts.

To make up

Make up as for Orange Spotted Fish, but omit fringe and spots and use black yarn for side fins.

Top fin

Using black yarn and blunt-ended yarn needle, work overcast stitches over top fin as shown.

BLACK AND WHITE FISH

To make fish

Beg at tail end of fish as foll:
Using 3¼mm (US size 3) needles and black yarn, cast on 4 sts.

Shape tail

Work tail in st st as foll:

Row 1 (RS) K to end.

Row 2 (inc row) P to last st, P into front and back of st to inc one st—called *Pfb*. (5 sts)

Rep last 2 rows once more, so ending with a WS (P) row. (6 sts)

Knit 1 row.

Shape body

Cont as foll:

Next row (inc row) (RS) Using white yarn, cast on and K 6 sts, K to end. (12 sts)

Using white yarn, purl 1 row.

Next row (inc row) Using black yarn,

Kfb, K to last st, Kfb. (14 sts)

Using black yarn, purl 1 row.

Next row (inc row) Using white yarn, Kfb, K to last st, Kfb. (16 sts)

Using white yarn, purl 1 row.

Next row (inc row) (RS) Using black yarn, Kfb, K to last st, Kfb. (18 sts)

Using black yarn, purl 1 row.

Rep last 2 rows twice more, so ending with a WS row. (22 sts)

Beg with a K row, work straight in st st, working in stripes as foll:

4 rows white, 3 rows black, 3 rows hot pink, so ending with a WS row.

Shape nose

Cont with hot pink yarn only as foll:

Next row (dec row) (RS) Cast off first 8 sts k-wise, K to last 8 sts, cast off last 8 sts and fasten off. (6 sts)

With WS facing, rejoin hot pink yarn and P to end.

Beg with a K row, work straight in st st for 4 rows, so ending with a WS row.

Next row (dec row) (WS) K2tog, K2, K2tog. (4 sts)

Break off yarn, leaving a long tail-end, then thread yarn end onto a blunt-ended yarn needle and pass yarn needle through rem 4 sts as they are slipped off knitting needle. Pull tight to gather sts and secure with a few sts.

Dorsal fin

Using 3¼mm (US size 3) needles and pale yellow yarn, cast on 7 sts, leaving a long tail-end of yarn for sewing in place. Purl 1 row.

Beg with a K row and working in st st, cast off 1 st at beg of each of next 4 rows, so ending with a WS row. (3 sts)

Beg with a K row, work straight in st st for 3 rows, so ending with a *RS* row.

Next row (WS) K2tog, K1.

Next row K2tog. Fasten off.

To make up

Make up as for Orange Spotted Fish, but omit fringe and spots and use orange yarn for eye. (For alternative side fins, using white yarn, work a short crochet chain for each fin and sew in place.)

Dorsal fin

Sew one row-end edge of dorsal fin to top of fish as shown.

BLUE SEAHORSE

To make seahorse

Beg at tail end of seahorse as foll:

Using 3¼mm (US size 3) needles and one strand of mid blue yarn and one strand of turquoise yarn held tog, cast on 3 sts.

Beg with a K, work 2 rows in st st, so ending with a WS row.

Shape tail and belly

Next row (inc row) (RS) K into front and back of st to inc one st—called *Kfb*—, K to last st, Kfb. (5 sts)

Beg with a P, work straight in st st for 2 rows, so ending with a *RS* row.

Next row (inc row) (WS) P into front and back of st to inc one st—called *Pfb*—, P to last st, Pfb. (7 sts)

Beg with a K, work 2 rows in st st, so ending with a WS row.

Next row (inc row) (RS) Kfb, K to last st, Kfb. (9 sts)

Beg with a P row, work straight in st st for 7 rows, so ending with a WS row.

Shape neck

Next row (dec row) (RS) K2tog, K to end. (8 sts)

Purl 1 row.

Rep last 2 rows once more (but work dec at end of first row instead of beg), so ending with a WS row. (7 sts)

Break off turquoise and mid blue yarns.

Shape head

Change to one strand of green yarn and beg with a K row, work straight in st st for 2 rows, so ending with a WS row.

Next row (dec row) (RS) K2tog, K3, K2tog. (5 sts)

Beg with a P row, work straight in st st 5 rows, so ending with a WS row.

Next row (dec row) (RS) K2tog, K1, K2tog. (3 sts)

Purl 1 row.

Shape mouth

Add one strand of hot pink yarn to one strand of green yarn (to double up with existing yarn) and knit 1 row.

Break off yarn, then thread yarn end onto a blunt-ended yarn needle and pass yarn needle through rem 3 sts as they are slipped off knitting needle. Pull tight to gather sts and form an O-shaped mouth.

one strand of hot pink yarn, cast on 6 sts.
Purl 1 row.

Next row (dec row) *K2tog, rep from
* to end.

Break off yarn, leaving a long
tail-end, then thread yarn end onto
a blunt-ended yarn needle and pass
yarn needle through rem 3 sts as they
are slipped off knitting needle. Pull to
gather sts loosely and use end to sew
to Seahorse.

To make up

Press pieces lightly on wrong side
following instructions on yarn label.
Using blunt-ended yarn needle and
matching yarn for all seams, sew seams
as follows:

Fold Seahorse in half lengthwise with
right sides together and sew seam,
leaving a small opening. Turn right
side out and insert filling. Sew opening
closed.

Sew head fin to top of head and
backbone fin to center of back as shown.

Eyes

Using blunt-ended yarn needle and
white yarn, work a satin stitch eye at
each side of head, then complete with
a black French knot in center.

PINK SEAHORSE

To make seahorse

Make as for Blue Seahorse, but use
one strand of hot pink yarn and one
strand of rust yarn held tog for body,
one strand of hot pink yarn for head,
and two strands of hot pink yarn
for mouth.

Backbone and head fins

Work as for Blue Seahorse, but
using light coral yarn.

Backbone fin

Using 3¼mm (US size 3) needles and
one strand of hot pink yarn, cast on
20 sts.
Purl 1 row.

Next row (dec row) *K2tog, rep from *
to end. (10 sts)
Purl 1 row.

Next row (dec row) *K2tog, rep

from * to end. (5 sts)
Break off yarn, leaving a long tail-end,
then thread yarn end onto a blunt-
ended yarn needle and pass yarn needle
through rem 5 sts as they are slipped off
knitting needle. Pull to gather sts loosely
and use end to sew to Seahorse.

Head fin

Using 3¼mm (US size 3) needles and

To make up

Make up as for Blue Seahorse.

CRAB

Body top

Using 3¼mm (US size 3) needles and one strand of yellow yarn and one strand of pale ochre yarn held tog, cast on 4 sts.

Working in garter st (knit every row), shape body top as foll:

Row 1 (inc row) (RS) K into front and back of st to inc one st—called *Kfb*—, K to last st, Kfb. (6 sts)

Row 2 K to end.

Rep rows 1 and 2 twice. (10 sts)

Row 7 (dec row) K2tog, K to last 2 sts, K2tog. (8 sts)

Row 8 K to end.

Rep rows 7 and 8 twice. (4 sts)

Cast off k-wise.

Underbody

Work as for body top, but using only one strand of white yarn.

Pincers (make 2)

Using 3¼mm (US size 3) needles and one strand of black yarn, cast on 2 sts. Break off black yarn, change to one strand of orange yarn and work in garter st as foll:

Row 1 (inc row) (RS) Kfb, K to last st, Kfb. (4 sts)

Row 2 K to end.

Rep rows 1 and 2 three times. (10 sts) Knit two rows.

Row 11 (dec row) K2tog, K to last 2 sts, K2tog. (8 sts)

Rows 12 and 13 K to end.

Row 14 Rep row 6. (6 sts)

Rows 15 and 16 K to end.

Row 17 Rep row 6. (4 sts)

Rows 18–20 K to end.

Cast off k-wise.

To make up

Do NOT press.

Using blunt-ended yarn needle and matching yarn for all seams, sew seams as follows:

With right sides together, backstitch body top to underbody, leaving an opening. Turn right side out. Lightly fill with toy filling and sew opening closed.

Eyes

Using one strand of black yarn, work one French knot for each eye, positioning them at cast-off edge. Fold each pincer in half lengthwise and sew seam. Sew pincers to body next to eyes.

Legs

For legs, cut eight strands of light coral 4-ply cotton yarn, each 10cm/4in long. Fold one strand in half, thread fold through a blunt-ended yarn needle and slide needle along to opposite end of yarn. Insert needle in and out through seam next to cast-on edge at back of crab and as needle emerges, pass it through loop at folded end of strand. Pull loop down to body to secure, then slip off needle. Sew on remaining seven strands like this, four on each side of body. Knot each pair of strands together 3cm/1¼in from body, then trim off ends 1cm/⅜in from knot.

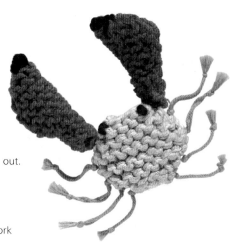

Dolphin

This is the most playable toy I have ever made. He moves just like a dolphin and has proven to be an absolute favorite. All knit using a medium yarn, he takes no time at all.

Finished size

Completed toy measures approximately 45cm (17¾in) from tip of nose to end of tail.

Yarn

Main body and fins: One 50g/1¾oz ball of Rowan *RYC Cashcotton DK* in main color MC (mid blue/Cool 601) and small amount of each in A (White 600), B (turquoise/Pool 602), C (pink/Sweet 501), and D (Black 607); *or other DK-weight (US light-worsted-weight) yarn in 5 colors of choice*

Side markings: Small amount of Rowan *RYC Cashsoft Baby DK* in E (pale blue/Cloud 805) *or other DK-weight (US light-worsted-weight) yarn in color of choice*

Extras

Polyester toy filling

Needles

Pair of 3¾mm (US size 5) knitting needles
Blunt-ended yarn sewing needle

Tension/gauge

22 sts and 40 rows to 10cm/4in measured over garter st using 3¾mm (US size 5) needles and yarn MC.

DOLPHIN

Body

Beg body of Dolphin at nose end as foll:
Using 3¾mm (US size 5) needles and yarn MC (mid blue), cast on 3 sts.

Shape nose

Working in garter st (knit every row), shape nose as foll:

Row 1 (inc row) *K into front and back of st to inc one st—called *Kfb*—, rep from * to end. (6 sts)

Row 2 K to end.

Row 3 (inc row) *Kfb, rep from * to end. (12 sts)

Rep last 2 rows once more. (24 sts)

Work straight in garter st for 14 rows.

Cont in garter st, cast off 6 sts at beg of each of next 2 rows. (12 sts)

This completes nose section.

Shape head

Next row (inc row) *Kfb, rep from * to end. (24 sts)

Work straight in garter st for 3 rows.

Next row (inc row) *Kfb, rep from * to end. (48 sts)

Work straight in garter st until toy measures 15cm/6in from cast-on edge.

Next row (dec row) [K2, K2tog] twice, K to last 8 sts, [K2tog, K2] twice. (44 sts)

Work straight in garter st for 3 rows.

Rep last 4 rows once more. (40 sts)

Next row (dec row) [K2, K2tog] twice, K to last 8 sts, [K2tog, K2] twice. (36 sts)

Work straight in garter st until toy measures 28cm/11in from cast-on edge.

Shape tail

Next row (dec row) K2tog, K to last 2 sts, K2tog. (34 sts)

Knit 1 row.

Rep last 2 rows twice more. (30 sts)

Shape end of tail

Next row (dec row) (WS) P2tog, P6, K14, P6, P2tog. (28 sts)

Knit 1 row.

Next row P7, K14, P7.

Knit 1 row.

Rep last 2 rows once more.

Next row (dec row) P2tog, P5, K14, P5, P2tog. (26 sts)

Knit 1 row.

Rep last 2 rows twice more. (22 sts)

Next row *K2tog, rep from * to end. (11 sts)

Break off yarn, leaving a long tail-end, then thread yarn end onto a blunt-ended yarn needle and pass yarn needle through sts as they are slipped off knitting needle. Pull tight to gather sts and secure with a few sts.

Mouth gusset

Using 3¾mm (US size 5) needles and yarn A (white), cast on 3 sts.

Shape jaw

Working in garter st, shape jaw as foll:

Making the **Dolphin**

Row 1 (inc row) *Kfb, rep from * to end. (6 sts)

Row 2 K to end.

Row 3 (inc row) *Kfb, rep from * to end. (12 sts)

Rep last 2 rows once more. (24 sts)

Work straight in garter st for 16 rows.

Cont in garter st, cast off 6 sts at beg of each of next 2 rows. (12 sts)

This completes jaw section.

Shape throat section

Change to st st and cont as foll:

Purl 1 row.

Next row (dec row) (RS) K2tog, K to last 2 sts, K2tog. (10 sts)

Rep last 2 rows 3 times more. (4 sts)

Purl 1 row.

Next row (dec row) [K2tog] twice. (2 sts)

Cast off p-wise.

Back side fins (make 4)

Using 3¾mm (US size 5) needles and yarn B (turquoise), cast on 5 sts.

Rib row 1 [K1, P1] twice, K1.

Rib row 2 [P1, K1] twice, P1.

Last 2 rows form K1, P1 rib patt.

Keeping K1, P1 rib correct as set throughout, beg shaping fins as foll:

Rib row 3 (inc row) Work into front and back of first st to inc 1 st, work in rib to last st, work into front and back of next st to inc 1 st. (7 sts)

Rib row 4 Work in rib to end.

Rep last 2 rows 6 times more. (19 sts)

Next row (inc row) Work into front and back of first st to inc 1 st, work in rib to last st, work into front and back of next st to inc 1 st. (21 sts)

Work straight in rib for 12 rows.

Next row (dec row) Work first 2 sts tog, work in rib to last 2 sts, work last 2 sts tog. (19 sts)

Next row Work in rib to end.

Rep last 2 rows 6 times more. (7 sts)

Next row (dec row) Work first 2 sts tog, work in rib to last 2 sts, work last 2 sts tog. (5 sts)

Next row K2tog, K1, K2tog. (3 sts)

Cast off.

Front side fins (make 2)

Using 3¾mm (US size 5) needles and yarn C (pink), cast on 14 sts.

Row 1 (inc row) *Kfb, rep from * to end. (28 sts)

Work straight in garter st for 3 rows.

Cont in garter st, decreasing as foll:

Next row K2tog, K to end. (27 sts)

Rep last row 3 times more. (24 sts)

Next row K2tog, K to last 2 sts, K2tog. (22 sts)

Rep last row 7 times more. (8 sts)

Next row *K2tog, rep from * to end. (4 sts)

Break off yarn leaving a long tail-end, then thread yarn end onto a blunt-ended yarn needle and pass yarn needle through sts as they are slipped off knitting needle. Pull tight to gather and secure with a few sts.

Large top fin

Using 3¾mm (US size 5) needles and yarn D (black), cast on 18 sts.

Row 1 (inc row) *Kfb, rep from * to end. (36 sts)

Work 6 rows in garter st.

Break off yarn D and change to yarn MC (mid blue).

Cont in garter st, decreasing as foll:

Next row K2tog, K to end. (35 sts)

Rep last row 3 times more. (32 sts)

Next row K2tog, K to last 2 sts, K2tog. (30 sts)

Rep last row 5 times more. (20 sts)

Break off yarn MC and change to yarn E (pale blue).

Next row K2tog, K to last 2 sts, K2tog. (28 sts)

Rep last row 8 times more. (12 sts)

Next row *K2tog, rep from * to end. (6 sts)

Break off yarn leaving a long tail-end, then thread yarn end onto a blunt-ended yarn needle and pass yarn needle through sts as they are slipped off knitting needle. Pull tight to gather sts and secure with a few sts.

Side markings (make 2)

Using 3¾mm (US size 5) needles and yarn E (pale blue), cast on 3 sts.

Row 1 (inc row) (RS) *Kfb, rep from * to end. (6 sts)

Beg with a P row, work straight in st st for 7 rows, so ending with a WS row.

Next row (inc row) (RS) *Kfb, K to last st, Kfb. (8 sts)

Beg with a P row, work straight in st st for 7 rows, so ending with a WS row.

Next row (inc row) (RS) *Kfb, K to last st, Kfb. (10 sts)

**Beg with a P row, work straight in st st for 4 rows, so ending with a *RS* row.

Next row (inc row) (WS) Pfb, P to last st, Pfb.** (12 sts)

Beg with a K row, work straight in st st for 4 rows, so ending with a WS row.

Next row (inc row) (RS) Kfb, K to last st, Kfb. (14 sts)

Rep from ** to ** once more, so ending with a *RS* row. (16 sts)

Beg with a K row, work straight in st st for 3 rows, so ending with a RS row.

Next row (dec row) (WS) P2tog, P to last 2 sts, P2tog. (14 sts).

Next row (dec row) K2tog, K to last 2 sts, K2tog. (12 sts)

Rep last 2 rows twice more. (4 sts)

Next row [K2 tog] twice. (2 sts)

Cast off p-wise.

To make up

Press two stocking/stockinette stitch side markings and areas of stocking/stockinette stitch on body lightly on wrong side, following instructions on yarn label.

Do NOT press garter stitch or ribbed pieces.

Body and mouth gusset

Using blunt-ended yarn needle and matching yarn for all seams, sew seams as follows:

Begin by sewing nose seam. To do this, fold nose at beginning of body in half lengthwise so that right sides are facing. Sew nose seam between nose cast-off edge and cast-on edge of body. Turn nose section right side out.

With right sides together, sew seam along belly of Dolphin, leaving head section open to insert throat section of mouth gusset. Turn right side out.

Sew jaw seam on mouth gusset as for nose seam and turn jaw right side out. Sew mouth gusset to body along shaped edges of throat section, leaving cast-off edges inside mouth open. Insert toy filling into body through mouth. Lightly fill nose section, but leave jaw section (white) unfilled. Overcast stitch seam inside mouth, joining two cast-off edges and aligning center seams.

To enhance shape of tail, work a line of backstitch through tail, separating stocking/stockinette stitch and garter stitch sections.

Eyes and blow hole

Using yarn D (black) and blunt-ended yarn needle, work satin stitch eyes, positioning as shown. Work a single French knot in yarn D for a blow hole at top of head (about 10cm/4in from nose tip).

Back side fins

Sew together turquoise back side fins in pairs, leaving a small opening for inserting toy filling. Lightly fill two fins with toy filling. Sew each opening closed. Sew fins to back of body, positioning as shown.

Front side fins

Fold each pink front side fin in half, with row-end edges together and wrong sides facing. Overcast stitch fin seam, leaving a small opening for inserting toy filling. Sew opening closed. Sew fins to body, with folded edge of fin facing towards tail end of Dolphin and positioning as shown.

Large top fin

Sew seam on large top fin as for front side fins, lightly filling fin before completing seam. Sew to top of body with seamed edge facing nose.

Side markings

Overcast stitch side marking shapes to sides of Dolphin's body, positioning as shown.

Templates

Use the patterns and templates on these three pages to make the sewn garments and accessories, following the instructions given here and in each project.

Where possible, the patterns and templates are printed at the correct size, but some will need to be enlarged on a photocopier, for which the appropriate enlargement factor is given.

Note that some of the templates combine layers of different shapes, each one in a different color. Also, where necessary there is a guide line to show where each of the pieces are to be placed.

Transferring patterns

Photocopy the pattern piece or template, enlarging it if necessary to the size specified. Take a note of how many pieces of fabric you need to cut for each pattern piece. Pin the pattern pieces to the chosen fabric, taking care to align the grainline arrow with the straight grain of the fabric and, if necessary, place any fold lines on a fold in the fabric. Cut out each shape along the outer line. Transfer any dots, notches, or other markings to the fabric.

Eyes, nose, and mouths

All the templates below are life size (100%). For each doll, cut two of each inner and outer eye and one mouth. The large eye and nostril at the top left (fig 1) are for the horses. The eye and mouth at the top right (fig 2) are for the girl dolls – the Princess, Fairy, and Mermaid. The small eye and mouth (fig 3) are for the Baby Fairy. The eye at the bottom right (fig 4) is for the Cowboy and Pirate, as are the outlines for the nose and mouth.

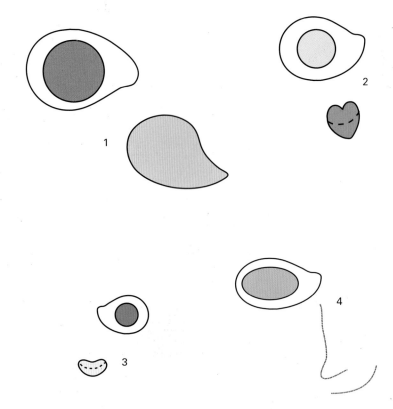

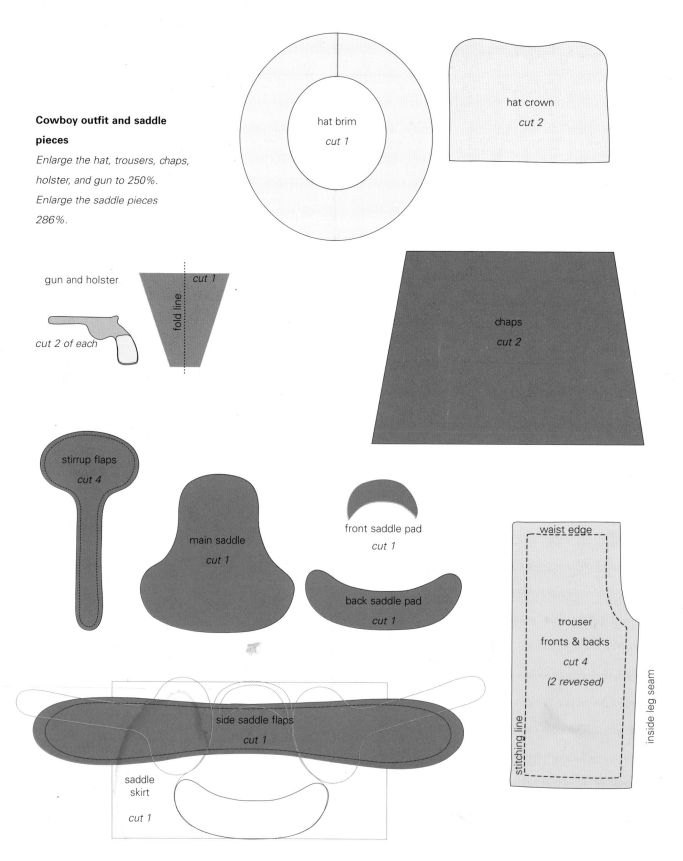

Cowboy outfit and saddle pieces

Enlarge the hat, trousers, chaps, holster, and gun to 250%. Enlarge the saddle pieces 286%.

hat brim
cut 1

hat crown
cut 2

gun and holster

cut 2 of each

cut 1

fold line

chaps
cut 2

stirrup flaps
cut 4

main saddle
cut 1

front saddle pad
cut 1

back saddle pad
cut 1

waist edge

trouser
fronts & backs
cut 4
(2 reversed)

stitching line

inside leg seam

side saddle flaps
cut 1

saddle
skirt

cut 1

Templates

Dinghy

The chart below is for the sail on the Dinghy, on page 86.

Each square on the chart represents one stitch; each row of squares – a row of stitches. Swiss darn/duplicate stitch the motif on the sail.

Fairy wings

Enlarge the wing templates 250%.

The larger wing is for the Fairy on page 44; the smaller for the Baby Fairy, on page 50.

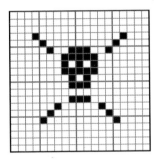

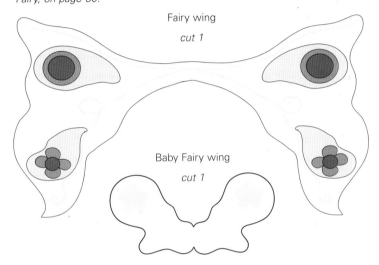

Fairy wing

cut 1

Baby Fairy wing

cut 1

Acknowledgments

A big thank you to all involved in this book at MB, especially Anna Sanderson and her unfailing support and confidence.

To Sally Harding, a marvel of an editor and author – I love your books Sally, thanks for helping me on mine.

Thanks to John, my husband for his beautiful photography; what fun we had on the beach with our children – the models – thanks Harry, May, and James for your patience and loveliness!

And last but not least all the bloggers on the babes site – all creative geniuses.